The
Undocumented
Americans

The Undocumented Americans

Karla Cornejo Villavicencio

Swift

Swift Press

First published in the United States of America by Penguin Random House 2020
First published in Great Britain by Swift Press 2021

1 3 5 7 9 8 6 4 2

The Undocumented Americans is a work of non-fiction.
Some names and identifying details have been changed.

Book design by Caroline Cunningham
Offset by Tetragon, London
Printed in England by CPI Group (UK) Ltd, Croydon, CR0 4YY

A CIP catalogue record for this book is available from the British Library

ISBN: 978-1-80075-039-5
eISBN: 978-1-80075-040-1

Chinga la Migra

A place belongs forever to whoever claims it
hardest, remembers it most obsessively,
wrenches it from itself, shapes it, renders it,
loves it so radically that he remakes it in his
own image.

—Joan Didion, *The White Album*

In memory of Claudia Goméz Gonzáles

CONTENTS

———— ⋄ ⋄ ⋄ ————

INTRODUCTION   xiii

CHAPTER 1: Staten Island   3

CHAPTER 2: Ground Zero   31

CHAPTER 3: Miami   57

CHAPTER 4: Flint   95

CHAPTER 5: Cleveland   118

CHAPTER 6: New Haven   147

ACKNOWLEDGMENTS   173

NOTES   177

INTRODUCTION

On the night of the 2016 presidential election, I spent a long time deciding what to wear. I'd be staying home to watch the returns with my partner, but the Comey letter had come out in mid-October and I was convinced Trump was going to win. I'd always admired the women on the *Titanic* who reportedly drowned wearing their finest clothing and furs and jewels and the violinists who kept playing even as the ship sank. I wore a burgundy velvet dress with sheer lace back paneling, a ribbon in my hair, red lipstick, and a leopard-print faux fur coat over my shoulders. I poured myself a goblet of wine. I understood that night would be my end, but I would not be ushered to an internment camp in sweatpants. The returns hadn't finished coming in when my father, who is undocumented, called me to tell me it was the end times. I threw myself into bed without washing off my makeup, without brushing my teeth. I had a four a.m. wake-up call.

A few hours later, I took a bunch of trains to New Jersey to meet an oceanographer I was profiling for a New York magazine. We took a boat into the Hudson and sped by the feet of the Statue of Liberty. "Fuck," I said. "This will appear sentimental." Still, I asked him to take my picture in front of it, and I smiled at the camera, the strong winds blowing my hair in my face.

It seemed safe, somehow, to be there, at Lady Liberty's feet. I got off the boat and, on my phone, emailed an agent I'd been friendly with since I was a kid and told him I was ready to write the book. *The* book. And he said okay.

The book. When I was a senior at Harvard, I wrote an anonymous essay for *The Daily Beast* about what they wanted to call "my dirty little secret"—that I was undocumented. It got me some attention—it was a different time—and agents wrote asking me if I wanted to write a memoir. A news program asked to film me while I fucking packed up my dorm, to show, I guess, that I was leaving Harvard without any plans, without even the promise of a career, which was the crux of my essay.

This was before DACA.

I was angry. A *memoir*? I was twenty-one. I wasn't fucking Barbra Streisand. I had been writing professionally since I was fifteen, but only about music—I wanted to be the guy in *High Fidelity*—and I didn't want my first book to be a rueful tale about being a sickly Victorian orphan with tuberculosis who didn't have a Social Security number, which is what the agents all wanted. The guy who eventually ended up becoming my agent respected that, did not find an interchangeable immigrant to publish a sad book, read everything I would write over the next seven years, and we kept in touch. I was the first person who wrote him on the morning of November 9, 2016.

That morning, I received a bunch of emails from people who were really freaked out about Trump winning and the emails essentially were offers to hide me in their second houses in Vermont or the woods somewhere, or stay in their basements. "Shit," I told my partner. "They're trying to Anne Frank me." By this point, I had been pursuing a PhD at Yale because I needed the health insurance and had read lots of books about migrants and I hated a good number of the texts. I couldn't see my family in them, because I saw my parents as more than laborers, as more than sufferers or dreamers. I thought I could write something better, something that rang true. And I thought that I was the best person to do it. I was just crazy enough. Because if you're going to write a book about undocumented immigrants in America, the story, the full story, you have to be a little bit crazy. And you certainly can't be enamored by America, not still. That disqualifies you.

This book is not a traditional nonfiction book. Names of persons have all been changed. Names of places have all been changed. Physical descriptions have all been changed. Or have they? I took notes by hand during interviews; after the legal review, I destroyed the notes. I chose not to use a recorder because I did not want to intimidate my subjects. Children of immigrants whose parents do not speak English learn how to interpret very young, and I honored that rite of passage and skill by translating the interviews on the spot. I approached translating the way a literary translator would approach translating a poem, not the way someone would approach translating a business letter. I hate the way journalists translate the words of Spanish speakers in their stories. They transliterate, and make us sound dumb, like we all have a first-grade vocabulary. I found my subjects to be warm, funny, dry, evasive, philosophical, weird, annoying, etc., and I tried to convey that tone in the translations.

When you are an undocumented immigrant with undocumented family, writing about undocumented immigrants—and I can only speak for myself and my ghosts—it feels unethical to put on the drag of a journalist. It is also painful to focus on the art, but impossible to process the world as anything but art. The slightest gust of the wind bruises—Trump's voice, Stephen Miller's face, the red hat, but also before that, the deli counter, the construction corner, the hotel room, the dishwashing station, the dollar store, the late-night English classes at the local community college—and it's a pain I am sure is felt by the eleven million undocumented, so I write as if it were. I attempt to write from a place of shared trauma, shared memories, shared pain. This is a snapshot in time, a high-energy imaging of trauma brain.

This book is a work of creative nonfiction, rooted in careful reporting, translated as poetry, shared by chosen family, and sometimes hard to read. Maybe you won't like it. I didn't write it for you to *like* it. And I did not set out to write anything inspirational, which is why there are no stories of DREAMers. They are commendable young people, and I truly owe them my life, but they occupy outsize attention in our politics. I wanted to tell the stories of people who work as day laborers, housekeepers, construction workers, dog walkers, deliverymen, people who don't inspire hashtags or T-shirts, but I wanted to learn about them as the weirdos we all are outside of our jobs.

This book is for everybody who wants to step away from the buzzwords in immigration, the talking heads, the kids in graduation caps and gowns, and read about the people underground. Not heroes. Randoms. People. Characters.

This book is for young immigrants and children of immigrants. I want them to read this book and feel what I imagine young people must have felt when they heard Nirvana's "Smells Like Teen Spirit" for the first time in Seattle in 1991. I grew up a Jehovah's Witness, and I remember what I felt listening to "Smells Like Teen Spirit" for the first time.

I went into the bathroom and chopped off my hair with my mom's fabric scissors and then messaged a boy who was not a Jehovah's Witness (not allowed) and told him to meet me at the Virgin Megastore in Times Square to give me my first kiss. This book will give you permission to let go. This book will give you permission to be free. This book will move you to be punk, when you need to be punk; y hermanxs, it's time to fuck some shit up.

Karla Cornejo Villavicenio

The
Undocumented
Americans

CHAPTER 1

Staten Island

AUGUST 1, 2019

If you ask my mother where she's from, she's 100 percent going to say she's from the Kingdom of God, because she does not like to say that she's from Ecuador, Ecuador being one of the few South American countries that has not especially out-done itself on the international stage—magical realism basi-cally skipped over it, as did the military dictatorship craze of the 1970s and 1980s, plus there are no world-famous Ecuadorians to speak of other than the fool who housed Julian Assange at the embassy in London (the president) and Christina Aguilera's fa-ther, who was a domestic abuser. If you ask my father where he is from, he will definitely say Ecuador because he is sentimental about the country for reasons he's working out in therapy. But if you push them, I mean *really* push them, they're both going to say they're from New York. If you ask them if they feel Ameri-can because you're a little narc who wants to prove your blood runs red, white, and blue, they're going to say *No, we feel like*

New Yorkers. We really do, too. My family has lived in Brooklyn and Queens a combined ninety-seven years. My dad drove a cab back when East New York was still gang country, and he had to fold his body into a little origami swan and hide under his steering wheel during cross fires in the middle of the day while he ate a jumbo slice of pizza. Times have changed but my parents haven't. My dad sees struggling bodegas and he says they're fronts. For what? Money laundering. For whom? *The mob.* My mother wants my brother and me to wear pastels all year round to avoid being seen as taking sides in the little tiff between the Bloods and the Crips.

My parents are New Yorkers to the core. Despite how close we are, we've talked very little about their first days in New York or about their decision to choose New York, or even the United States, as a destination. It's not that I haven't asked my parents why they came to the United States. It's that the answer isn't as morally satisfying as most people's answers are— a decapitated family member, famine—and I never press them for more details because I don't want to apply pressure on a bruise.

The story as far as I know it goes something like this: My parents had just gotten married in Cotopaxi, Ecuador, and their small autobody business was not doing well. Then my dad got into a car crash where he broke his jaw, and they had to borrow money from my father's family, who are bad, greedy people. The idea of coming to America to work for a year to make just enough money to pay off the debt came up and it seemed like a good idea. My father's family asked to keep me, eighteen months old at the time, as collateral. And that's what my parents did. That's about as much as I know.

You may be wondering why my parents agreed to leave me as
an economic assurance, but the truth is I have not had this conversation with them. I've never thought about it enough to ask.
The whole truth is that if I was a young mother—if I was *me* as
a young mother, unparented, ambitious, at my sexual prime—
I think I would be thrilled to leave my child for "exactly a year,"
as they said it would be, which is what the plan was. I never had
to forgive my mom.

My dad? My dadmydadmydad was my earliest memory. He
was dressed in a powder-blue sweater. He was walking into a
big airplane. I looked out from a window and my dad was walking away and, in my hand, I carried a Ziploc bag full of coins. I
don't know. It's been almost thirty years. It doesn't matter anymore.

My parents didn't come back after a year. They didn't stay in
America because they were making so much money that they
became greedy. They were barely making ends meet. Years
passed. When I was four years old, going to school in Ecuador,
teachers began to comment on how gifted I was. My parents
knew Ecuador was not the place for a gifted girl—the gender
politics were too fucked up—and they wanted me to have all the
educational opportunities they hadn't had. So that's when they
brought me to New York to enroll me in Catholic school, but no
matter how hard they both worked to make tuition, they fell
short. Then one day—I think I was in the fourth grade—the
school bursar called me into his office and explained that there
was an elderly billionairess who lived in upstate New York who
had heard about me and was impressed. He told her my family
was poor and might have to pull me from the school. (Okay, so
in this scenario the tragedy would have been that I'd have to go

to the local public school, which was not a great school, but just so we're on the same page, I support public schools and I would have been fine.) So she came up with a proposition. She'd pay for most of my tuition if I kept up my grades and wrote her letters.

That was the first time in my life I'd have a benefactor, but it would not be my last. When I was at Harvard, a very successful Wall Street man who knew me from an educational NGO we both belonged to—he as a supporter, me as a supported—learned I was undocumented and could not legally hold a work-study job, so every semester he wrote me a modest check. In the notes section he cheekily wrote "beer money"—the joke being that I wouldn't really drink until I was twenty-one—but every semester I used it for books, winter coats for those fucking Boston winters, money I couldn't ask my parents for because they didn't have any to give. I wrote him regular emails about my life at Harvard and my budding success as a published writer. He was always appropriate and boundaried. I had read obsessively about artists since I was a kid and considered myself an artist since I was a kid so I didn't feel weird about older, wealthy white people giving me money in exchange for grades or writing. It was *patronage*. They were Gertrude Stein and I was a young Hemingway. I was *Van Gogh*, crazy and broken. I truly did not have any racial anxieties about this, thank god. That kind of thing could really fuck a kid up.

I'm a New York City kid, but although the first five years of my time in America were spent in Brooklyn, if we're going to be real, I'm *from* Queens. Queens is the most diverse borough in the city. This might sound like a romanticized ghetto painting, but when I walk through my neighborhood, a Polish child with a toy gun will shoot at my head and say the same undecipherable word over and over; a Puerto Rican kid will rap along to a song on his phone and turn it up as loud as necessary to make out the lyrics, even rapping along to some N-words; some Egyptian teenagers will refuse to move out of my way as I'm simply trying to cross the street; and some Mexican guys will invite me to join a pyramid scheme. But none of us will try to take any rights away from one another. We don't have potlucks, but we live in peace. We go to the same street fairs.

The other boroughs are less diverse, but I found that the same thing is basically true. Except for one borough that I was always curious about—Staten Island, New York's richest, whitest, most suburban borough. It is almost 80 percent white. By way of comparison, Brooklyn and Queens are just less than half white, the Bronx is 45 percent white, and even Manhattan is only 65 percent white. Staten Island is geographically isolated— you can't take the subway there from the city—and, I don't know, man, there isn't a lot of shared goodwill between islanders and city residents. It's not like we're unaware. They've literally tried to secede from New York City and form their own city or join *New Jersey*. In June 1989, the New York State legislature gave Staten Island residents the right to decide on secession, and in November 1993, 65 percent of voters voted yes. Governor Mario Cuomo insisted that the referendum be approved by the state legislature, where it was defeated, but the desire continued to bubble just beneath the surface for years, so even after the world was rocked by Brexit, you had local island politicians posting on social media about how inspiring an event it was. Staten Island is the city's most conservative borough, pretty reliably Republican, the only borough in New York City to go for Donald Trump in the 2016 presidential election. It's also the borough where Eric Garner was killed in a choke hold at the hands of NYPD officer Daniel Pantaleo. A Staten Island grand jury declined to indict Pantaleo for murder.

I learned about all of this later. But the first time Staten Island really entered my consciousness was when there were news reports about hate crimes against Latinx people when I was a kid. This was the only context in which Staten Island was mentioned on Spanish nightly news—Mexican immigrants as victims of hate crimes at the hands of young black men, a cruel reminder of the rift between our communities. There was fifty-two-year-old Alejandro Galindo, who was walking his bicycle home from his dishwashing job and was attacked by four men who didn't take anything. There was eighteen-year-old Christian Vázquez, who was attacked by five men as he was coming home from his job as a busboy. They beat him and took jewelry and a measly ten dollars from him as they yelled anti-Mexican slurs. There was twenty-six-year-old Rodolfo Olmedo, jumped by four men on his way back from a club. They beat him with a baseball bat, a metal chain, and wooden planks. "We believe at this time that they selected this victim either in whole or in substantial part because he was a Mexican," Richmond County district attorney Daniel Donovan said.

I headed to Staten Island to report on the lives of undocumented day laborers in early 2017—it was close to where I lived in New Haven, and I was terrified about Trump having just assumed office. I was scared for all immigrants and felt guilty about myself as a so-called DREAMer. I was on DACA and I was afraid there'd be a raid. I was afraid that in any situation

where there were large groups of undocumented people con-
gregated, there could be a raid. My first trip there, I took a taxi
from the Newark train station, about a thirty-minute drive, to
the neighborhood of Silver View, home to one of the oldest day
laborer corners in New York City. I got carsick, so I closed my
eyes and filled the time with a mental rosary chain of short
prayers to god, out of whose favor I had fallen years ago. I rested
my head on the window and asked him to protect my family
first, and if he had some goodwill left over, I prayed that there
wouldn't be a raid on the warehouse where I was going that
night.

Before visiting Staten Island, I'd never met a day laborer. To
me, a city girl who knew undocumented men mostly as restaurant workers, day laborers seemed like an almost mythical ar-
chetype, groups of brown men huddled at the crack of dawn on
street corners next to truck rental lots and hardware super-
stores and lumberyards. Historically, legislators and immigration advocates have parted the sea of the undocumented with a
splintered staff—working brown men and women on one side
and academically achieving young brown people on the other,
one a parasitic blight, the other heroic dreamers. Day laborers
weren't real to me, and what I had heard about them wasn't
good. *The New York Times* described their work as "idling on
street corners." They haven't had the best PR.

So who are they? There are varied estimates of the number
of day laborers in New York City, from a little under six thousand to more than ten thousand. A 2006 survey of day laborers,
who are mostly men, reports that 75 percent of respondents
identified as undocumented, two-thirds supported their families
with this line of work, 60 percent said day laboring was their

first job in the United States, and 85 percent were looking for more permanent jobs. They represent a wide range of skills, from muscle to flooring to woodwork to welding to painting to cement work to brickwork to carpentry to insulation to stucco to electrical work to just about everything else in the construction universe.

The typical place they find work is the street corner, where a delicate choreography takes place. One guy told me the exchange goes something like this: *A man pulls up in a truck and says, I need X done. If a person has that skill, he'll ask for a quote— how many hours, in what location, how much per hour. Sometimes while you are negotiating, two other workers willing to do the job for less jump into the truck and the employer shrugs and drives away. Sometimes a group piles onto the sides of the truck, and the employer gets spooked. They don't know us. It's the group that scares them.* If they're scared, they might hastily pick one or two guys, or they might drive away. An average of sixty workers gathers on each of the known street corners in Silver View every day. On a quiet day there might be three workers, on a busy day a hundred. They mostly get paid in cash, and the employers are free to do with and to them whatever they want.

The day laborers I meet are professionals, talking about the importance of negotiating rates and building networks through good work and recommendations. They call their employers patrones, a Spanish word that means "bosses" but with a colonial aftertaste, often do not get protective equipment, meal breaks, or even bathroom breaks. They have all experienced racist abuse and wage theft at the hand of their employers, are all owed thousands of dollars by white men who made them work for days, promised payment, then simply disappeared. Some days laborers are dropped off at remote locations to do work, then left there without a ride back, unpaid and helpless. The fact that *The New York Times* described them as "idling" infuriates me. What an offensive way to describe labor that requires standing in hellish heat or cold or rain from dawn until nightfall, negotiating in a language not your own, competing with your own friends for the same job, then performing it to perfection without the certainty of pay. Workers absorb exceptional emotional and physical stress every day and, because they are undocumented, they're on their own, with no workplace protections, no regulations, and no collective bargaining.

This is where the worker centers come in. Worker centers were established to formalize this very informal sector of day laboring. There are now more than sixty-three worker centers across the country. Colectiva Por Fin is a storefront nonprofit on Staten Island that since 1997 has provided practical advocacy, representation, and training for day laborers and the immigrant community on the island at large. It sits on Silver View Road along with Nuestra Calle, another worker center, right near the busy street corners where day laborers generally congregate, and they make a world of difference for the men. First, they are indoors, so the men don't have to stand outside for hours on end in extreme weather. The centers provide restrooms, water, coffee, phone chargers, and dispatchers. Dispatchers serve as bilingual intermediaries between workers and employers, cementing transactions and preventing abuses or irregularities. It's a stressful job.

Santiago, a dispatcher at Colectiva Por Fin, is a U.S. citizen born to Mexican parents. Workers collectively set the rates for particular jobs annually or semiannually, and Santiago's job is to make sure those rates are honored and workers aren't drawn into potentially abusive arrangements. "Some employers think that exploiting them might be easy because they are undocumented," he tells me. Santiago is just twenty-five years old.

I'm attending a monthly meeting at Colectiva Por Fin on my first night on Staten Island. The room is small but as more men come in, it seems to double and triple in size. On the wall, migrants are celebrated through art that strikes me as deeply annoying, mostly the word "migrant" reconfigured as butterflies. I fucking hate thinking of migrants as butterflies. Butterflies can't fuck a bitch up. Tonight, about fifty men end up gathering in the room, plus a couple of women, including a young, white female pastor who works for Project Hospitality, the parent nonprofit. The executive director of Colectiva Por Fin is here, an Argentine man named Simón Torres. He is new and the men are still making up their minds about him. There are two African American day laborers at the meeting and an older white man with a shock of white hair and mustache. His name is Charles and he is here as an organizer from AmeriCorps. Because of these three people, the meeting is conducted bilingually by Santiago, effectively cutting the meeting shorter while making it feel longer at the same time. Out of the fifty Latinx workers, perhaps only a few are able to ascertain the fidelity of Santiago's translation.

The men here tonight are workers. For many years when I have heard nice people try to be respectful about describing undocumented people, I've heard them call us "undocumented workers" as a euphemism, as if there was something uncouth about being just an undocumented person standing with your hands clasped together or at your sides. I almost wish they'd called us

something rude like "crazy fuckin' Mexicans" because that's ac-
knowledging something about us beyond our usefulness—we're
crazy, we're Mexican, we're clearly unwanted!—but to describe
all of us, men, women, children, locally Instagram-famous teens,
queer puppeteers, all of us, as *workers* in order to make us palat-
able, my god. We were brown bodies made to labor, faces pix-
elated.

And here they are now, the workers. Some are very young,
just past their teens, and some are quite old, around seventy.
They are all wearing dirty work boots, but carefully kept. You
know how jeans come pre-ripped? That's how their boots look.
Dirty from work, pristine from care. The workers are very
brown, brown from their moms, browned from the sun. They
are short. But they are built. They look like they can walk on
burning coal, build a house, and open a bottle of beer with their
wedding rings.

When I scan the room, I see men lighter and darker than my
father, some older, most younger—they speak harsher, softer,
mumbling, or sung, but I see my father's face in their every one,
and I know that this astigmatism will always be with me; the
light will always fall this way. I think about the 2010 Arizona
immigration law known as the Support Our Law Enforcement
and Safe Neighborhoods Act, a.k.a. Arizona SB 1070, a.k.a. the
"papers please" law. It gave law enforcement officials the power
to approach anybody they suspected of being in the country illegally and ask for proof of legal documentation. That meant
they could stop anyone they thought *looked* undocumented.
Immigrant rights advocates furiously protested the law, chal-
lenging officials on how exactly they defined an *"undocumented
look."* But Vincent, my best friend from college, and I, two un-

documented kids, whispered to each other that even if the authorities "couldn't," we could pretty much almost always tell. The backpack my father carried on his commute to and from work, the one that held his earnings in cash, was a red flag. His black rubber orthopedic-looking shoes and his dark-blue jeans, immigrant-blue, an immigrant rinse. I offered to buy him new clothes but he said, Para que? Vincent offered to buy his dad a change of clothes for when he traveled home from his construction job but his dad said, Para que? too.

Santiago is an accomplished and artful translator. He works quickly and in real time and transmits tone impeccably. Charles from AmeriCorps gives a long-winded speech inviting the men to an upcoming church dinner. He keeps mentioning the president's name. In his translation, Santiago omits every mention of Trump. Charles says the dinner will feature American fare—"You're going to get to try American food; I promise you'll love it." That sentence too disappears in our young dispatcher's hands. Charles ends his speech by saying, "If things get worse, and I really, *really* don't think they will, Americans will come out and protect you." Santiago doesn't translate any of that either. He's pretty fucking good.

I ask Santiago where he learned to translate so well and he tells me that like many children of immigrants, he grew up interpreting for his parents at everything from PTA meetings to doctors' appointments. "It made me feel important," he says. "I was representing my parents." I tell Santiago I did the same thing, that we all did. I ask him why he omitted all mentions of Trump in the speech. "I didn't want to mention that guy," he says. "I wanted to make them feel safe."

STATEN ISLAND · 15

I ask why he completely omitted Charles's promise to protect them if things got bad.

"The reality is . . . it's not just Trump. Staten Island is a very conservative island. Charles might think it's not getting worse, but he is not going to be affected, unless they stop federal funding of his organization, and then he could lose his job. But the whole immigrant community has everything to lose."

But what about the guarantee that Americans would come to our rescue? I ask.

"Unless these Americans are lawyers or federal judges, I don't see how that's true," Santiago says.

A year and a half later, I've been to Staten Island so many times, I've lost count. I've grown attached to these men and look for any excuse to go back to learn more about the world the day laborers have created in the most anti-immigrant hood in the city. I've stood with them on street corners and sat with them in the worker centers, I've had coffee with them at Dunkin' Donuts, ate lunches with them at Ecuadorian restaurants they insist on paying for, delivered dinners for them to share in the worker center office, I've accompanied them to testify in City Hall, attended their Christmas party where none of them asked me to dance, went to their soccer matches, and spoke to them on the phone late at night. We texted Merry Christmas and Happy New Year to one another one minute after midnight. I blocked one of them on my phone because his intense loneliness was dark and desperate and it scared me. Come a blizzard in Connecticut, where I live now, and I think of how thin the lining is in their jackets; when the season changes and the pavement gets so hot that I don't walk my dog for longer than a few minutes out of concern for his soft padded feet, I think of how hot jet-black hair gets under the sun, like my brother's, like my father's, like mine. When I see acrylic blankets I think of them alone in their rented single rooms, and when my father visits me in my big apartment with all the natural light and big fiddle-leaf trees, I see them in his missing teeth and swollen hands. When my father lost his restaurant job of fifteen years, I asked one of my contacts from Colectiva if she knew of any jobs, and she said that he could go to the worker center at 7:00 A.M. to begin working as a day laborer. Imagine that. Day one as a day laborer, at age fifty-three.

Julián is fifty-two years old but looks much, much older. When I first meet him, he is sitting alone in the corner of the worker center wearing headphones as men wait for their assignments. His beanie is pulled over his eyebrows, covering the tops of his ears, actually almost half of his ears—he has small ears. Everyone else is talking and laughing. I ask him what he's listening to and he says, "Christian music to uplift the spirits." I persuade him to give me his number, but it takes a few conversations for him to open up. It's clear he has spent a lot of time alone with his thoughts. Many of the day laborers don't have family living with them on Staten Island and are lonely, so talking with me at the end of a long day from the tiny corners of their rooms is something they seem to like. With Julián, once he is ready, our conversations are like the opposite of bloodletting, the darker, thicker stuff coming out first, and then we work our way toward a light exchange about the weather before we hang up.

Julián didn't know a word of English when he came to the United States. His first meal in America was a bag of potato chips and a fifty-cent bottle of water. Remember those? He had nothing. He started work as a dishwasher at a restaurant two days later. His bosses were despots. They screamed at him, they swore. They had a rule that no outside food was allowed in the kitchen, but the only food the workers were allowed from the kitchen were eggs and potatoes. The cook was Latinx, like them, and he snuck them meat—cuts of chicken and steak—when the bosses turned their backs. "Pinche pendejo," the cook said.

The hours were long and pay was terrible, so he decided to give day laboring a try. On his first day, he was terrified. "I was scared to work because I did not know English," he says. "The employers yelled at me because I didn't. I would stand on the street corner with my friends, but because I was so scared, I sent them to do jobs that I was hired to do. I was scared that I could not speak English, and that in turn made me scared I could not do the job. But then I went to school."

When immigrants who did not go to school in this country— or at all—talk about their experiences at "school," they usually mean the local library or community college, where they take English classes. Every immigrant I know has embarked on involved attempts to learn English beyond just immersion. City University of New York officials recall a nighttime security guard at Brooklyn College telling them he saw immigrants line up before 4:00 A.M. for a 9:00 A.M. open registration for ESL classes. The nativist claim that immigrants do not want to learn

English makes me hysterical. Years ago, on a bus in Queens, an older woman bitterly spit out in my direction as I passed by, "I wish these people would just learn English." I had not been speaking—at all, in any language. I was holding a book, in English. In fact, I was home for the summer after my freshman year at Harvard, where I would win a writing award named after an eighteenth-century American transcendentalist—we both just happened to write in English. But it was summertime, and I wore short, thin, slutty things, so I was tan, a deeper brown than usual; my hair was so black it was almost navy. I think every immigrant in this country knows that you can eat English and digest it so well that you shit it out, and to some people, you will still not speak English.

I ask Julián what he'd like readers to know about him, and he immediately says, "Tell them I crossed the desert four times to see my children." The border was more porous at the time, and his children were in Mexico, so he headed home during the New York winter. He still needed a coyote for the crossing. At night in the desert it got so cold, he thought his skin would shatter like hard candy. During the day it was so hot, he thought demons had possessed him. He carried with him four gallons of water and a backpack with food. He wore construction boots, and his feet were covered in blisters. Once, he stayed behind with some people who'd gotten sick and the coyote just left them. "The coyotes are always drugged and drunk because they're afraid to do what they do sober," Julián explains. They survived by eating cans of peppers and drinking puddles. Two of them died. They threw up something green, then collapsed. He tried to help the living, but also didn't want to join the dead, so he did what he had to do.

Like most marriages divided by a border, his ended in separa-tion. He sent money to his kids in Mexico, but he was lonely in New York and he dreamed of having a new bouncing little brown baby, ideally a girl, and he wanted to raise her bilingual. That was the main thing he fantasized about at night, as he lay in the dark waiting for his exhausted body and his racing heart to catch up to each other so he could sleep: He dreamed of hav-ing a baby who would have a first word in Spanish—papi—and a first word in English—mommy. He'd give the baby an Ameri-can name and learn to pronounce it the right way. Maybe "Lin-coln," which was hard because your tongue had to be so sneaky in the middle of the word. He'd take Lincoln to all the Disney movies and at first he'd be able to follow just enough of the plot to not fall asleep, but eventually he'd get the jokes. He'd go to parent-teacher conferences and not rely on his kid to translate. No, he'd wear a suit and a tie and ask the tough questions him-self, so the little imp couldn't hide her naughtiness. "I think it would be beautiful to speak in English to your child," he says.

As time went on, it became clear he wasn't going to have this baby, and he got lonelier and lonelier. "You come here thinking of your kids, but the process changes you. You're transformed, and sometimes you can't get out of that place. Some people never knew their fathers. They have traumas from childhood, from the crossing, and they don't know how to handle those problems but they can buy a Corona." Soon, he started spending all of his time in bars, leaving them at dawn and going straight to work after. He'd send money home and spend the rest on al-cohol. He was consumed by guilt.

Then one night in January, he drank too much while he had the flu, and the combination of whiskey and a fever led to hallucinations, including one of being hunted down by police dogs. Julián tried to shake off the hallucinations but he couldn't. So he started screaming. Nobody came to his rescue because he was alone. He woke himself with his own screams, and upon waking he told god that if he let him have a peaceful sleep, he'd stop drinking.

"I don't know if it was a miracle, but since then I haven't wanted to go to bars anymore. I just want to work. What distracts me is work. What makes me happy is working. When I'm not working, I freak out."

If you left America, what would you miss? I ask him.

"I'd miss the money," Julián says.

Me too, I say.

We both laugh.

Joaquín also crossed the desert four times. His first time crossing began at nightfall. Five or six men covered in guns pick up the crossers in an old yellow truck, then drive them to a line in the sand where the narcos are waiting. You know they're narcos because they're wearing chains and their eyes are dead. You need a password to cross. The coyotes whisper the password, and the migrants get off the truck. They are dumped onto another truck. Only one coyote can go with them. *Were you scared?* I ask. "Are you kidding? I was terrified," Joaquín says. "They're *narcos.*"

They drive to a mountain. They dump the truck. *Time to climb the mountain,* putas. Joaquín isn't a thin man, but he'll be fine. He'll be fine! He exercises. I mean he wakes up every morning and does stretches while he does his morning prayers. Reach to the sky, now touch your toes, side to side. The mountain is steep, and it is hot, and his backpack is heavy. He climbs for about an hour imagining he is a guest on *Sábado Gigante* recounting his tale of rescuing a girl who fell into a well. Then his backpack straps break. Right at the seams—irreparable. His backpack, enormous, carries all his cans of food and water gallons, plus an extra layer of clothing for the freezing desert nights. Before he even thinks them, words rush into his mouth. They flood in there and all he has to do is vomit them. "Friends, I'm staying here." He's calling it. He's done. He hadn't even realized he's exhausted, but he allows himself to admit it. All he wanted was an out. In his mind he is going to sit down on the mountain and take a nap; finish the provisions in his backpack; have a feast of canned beans, saltines, and water; and then, after he's run out, sit there in the sun—it won't take very long to start dying. Eventually the animals will notice and they'll eat him and he'll let them. He'll put up some struggle, it's human nature. Hopefully he'll be so dehydrated by then that he won't even notice the tears in his flesh—it'll feel like paper cuts on a really bad sunburn, and to the bobcats he'll be jerky. "When you choose to die, you really have to decide to die," Joaquín tells me. But then, these two young guys—to this day he doesn't know their names—these guys step forward and get all up in his face like they're going to punch him. He takes a few steps back. They get in his space again. One of them thrusts forward, furious, and yanks Joaquín's backpack from him. "This is why you wanna die, 'mano?" Then the other one walks behind Joaquín and begins to push him by his shoulders. Up the mountain. Up the incline. Cursing under their breath. Joaquín chastises himself the whole time. *These kids don't want me dead so now I can't die.*

What do you do when your out was to die and now you can't die because you're living for total strangers? There was another mountain after the first one. And on the second mountain he grabbed back his backpack and walked right behind the coyotes. "And by the time we climbed down, I had gathered so much strength," he says. "I think about those kids all the time. I think about them every day. Every time there is a raid, I think about them." He knew they went to Las Vegas, but they could be anywhere now. They could be deported. They could be dead.

Joaquín's first steady job in New York was at a "boat company," which I took to mean a ferry service. He was on a boat on the Hudson River on September 11, 2001, when he saw the planes crash into the towers, and without even knowing what had happened, his boss rounded up the workers and told everyone to get ready to head into the city to help. By the time they arrived, the second tower had fallen and there was debris and dust everywhere. He couldn't even see where he was walking. The boats transported workers in and out of Ground Zero for two weeks, dressed in the yellow suits and masks generally used for oil spills; the workers and the boats were hosed down at night with a power wash. He feels proud of the work he did there. "They gave people who entered that zone an ID, and I remember the day we were supposed to hand that ID back. I couldn't return it. I just couldn't. I kept it as a memory that I worked at Ground Zero."

Then one day, out of the blue, the boat company owner gathered all of the Mexican workers. "I'm sorry but I can't work with you anymore. Immigration can find me, and they will fine me," he said. Then he made them sign some forms likely liberating the employers from any responsibility from suddenly firing them. Joaquín didn't read them before signing the documents. Neither did the other guys. "That's what I regret. I didn't take a photograph of those forms or make a copy of them. We didn't even read the letter." That was before Colectiva Por Fin, and their Know Your Rights training for day laborers. He insists he would never let someone do that to him again. "They have really opened my eyes to the rights of workers. I'm more awake than I was before and I wouldn't sign something again without reading it," he says.

After he was fired from the boat company, Joaquín arrived at the corner. He was now a day laborer.

Hurricane Sandy hit the night of October 29, 2014, at the precise moment the Atlantic Ocean and New York Harbor both reached full tide. High tide on that night meant the water levels along the southern coast were already elevated about five feet higher than usual. Furthermore, it was not only a high tide but a spring tide, meaning the moon was full and the tide, which operates along a cycle, was at its highest monthly point, about half a foot higher than the highest point of the high tide you would see during a normal storm. Once it picked up its full force, Sandy came through the East Coast a thousand miles wide, making it three times the size of Hurricane Katrina. It was a spectacle of wind and the ocean's fickle, maniacal force, and New York's man-made dunes and bulkheads only dulled the hurricane's mighty impact.

The Hurricane Katrina cleanup set the model for Hurricane Sandy. After Katrina, about half of the reconstruction crews in New Orleans were Latinx, and more than half of those were undocumented. They worked the most dangerous jobs for the lowest wages. They picked up dead bodies without gloves and masks. They waded waist-deep in toxic waters. During this same period, New Orleans mayor Ray Nagin asked a room of business leaders, "How do I make sure New Orleans is not over-run with Mexican workers?" There would be no way.

The first and biggest contractor to come on the scene after Sandy hit was AshBritt Environmental, now famous for having squandered $500 million in government contracts after Katrina, while charging 44 percent more than local contractors and paying subcontractors only $10 of every $23 it received per cubic yard, out of which the workers received their paltry wages. The company left behind two EPA-designated superfund sites.

But Sandy brought death before the contractors came. Most of the initial deaths were due to drowning. There were forty drowning deaths, and half happened in people's homes. Much of Staten Island ignored orders to evacuate because evacuation orders had also been issued for Hurricane Irene the year prior and then the storm swerved around Staten Island and landed up-state, leaving the boroughs intact. When the orders came this time, half of Staten Island was designated as Evacuation Zone A, meaning that half was especially vulnerable to flooding, and city officials targeted that area with phone calls, televised reminders, and door-to-door calls for evacuation. The community says National Guard members also went door-to-door in neighbor-hoods in the storm's path, but activists tell me that immigrants felt unsafe when they saw uniformed people knocking on doors at all hours, especially if they lacked papers.

The storm caused $62 billion in damages in the United States, killed 125 people, and left 7.5 million people without power. The city had not prepared for that kind of devastation and was slow to provide aid. Day laborers were among the first people on the ground to help. "In times of crisis, day laborers are often the first responders," one labor organizer told me.

Pedro Ituralde is a forty-one-year-old Chilean man who was the longtime executive director of Colectiva Por Fin and now leads Nuestra Calle. He had just come back from a trip to Chile when the storm hit. He sprang into action, organizing volunteer brigades of day laborers so that four or five brigades were on the ground at all times. They cleaned flooded basements, removed fallen branches and trees, repaired fences, waded in dirty waters up to their knees to remove furniture from houses, removed drywall, picked up debris, whatever needed to get done.

Every single day laborer I meet loves, trusts, and speaks adoringly of Pedro. He is an institution in immigrant Staten Island, something of a godfather figure despite his youth and the fact that he is openly gay, and this in the all-male Latinx day laborer community. I ask him how he maneuvers that. "I ask them if they've ever been discriminated against, and they all say yes," Pedro says. "So I tell them the LGBTQ community is discriminated against just like they are, and it is their job as people who have been hurt by prejudice to not hurt anyone else. And they all get it." It is the only sliver of personal information about himself that Pedro is willing to share in our three years of constant communication, visits, phone calls, emails, texts, and bribes in the form of midday cappuccinos and flans delivered to his office. He does not want the focus on himself.

Pedro was inspired to organize the storm volunteer brigades after hearing stories from Latinx New Yorkers who went to government-run restoration centers and were turned away by guards who told them, "You don't belong here," or, "You're not from here. I know you're lying." Occupy Sandy, a group made up of former Occupy Wall Street activists, donated supplies to the worker center—sleeping bags, batteries, toilet paper, and flashlights, as did Mexican pop superstar Thalía, who lives in New York and in a message of support called the day laborers "my brothers." The men stuffed the supplies into bright yellow drawstring bags with Colectiva Por Fin's logo on it. This was a team-building move proposed by Pedro, who is also known to make his team members do trust falls. The yellow bags became famous across the beachfront communities on Staten Island. Pedro tells me he heard a woman call into a local radio show to complain about the government's lack of response, saying the only people who had their shit together were the day laborers. "We helped two hundred and forty families," he says. "And that was the government's job."

Along the beach, Colectiva Por Fin set up a tent where they ran daily Occupational Safety and Health Administration (OSHA) trainings and offered vests and masks for laborers who needed replacements. The experience built goodwill in the community. The local precinct's police chief began coming to the Colectiva Por Fin offices to meet the men, and Pedro brought some day laborers to community council meetings. When community members said that they ruined the neighborhood by urinating in public or hollering at women, the men responded, "That may be one person. Look at me, look at us. Day laborers as a whole do not behave that way."

The first jobs after the storm hit were removal of garbage and debris, knocking down damaged walls or other large structures, and the removal of mold. Unlike most volunteers, day laborers had the skill set to do extensive renovation projects, including specialized work like painting, electrical wiring, and landscaping. Beyond helping those in need, the workers were networking, giving their neighbors a sampling of their skills in hopes of encouraging future working relationships, but many people just took the free labor and never contacted them again. Some home owners even failed to provide essential tools for cleanup, such as masks, or even mops and garbage bags, and volunteer workers had to bring their own.

Joaquín was one of the volunteers during Hurricane Sandy. At first, recovery days were workdays like any other. He woke up, bought a buttered roll and coffee with milk and sugar from the bodega (he only drinks his coffee black on weekends, the morning after he drinks beer), and went to work. He worked seven days a week. He is a big man, so first he helped residents get everything onto the street, anything that had been touched by salt water, mostly furniture. He went into a lot of basements, a little scared each time that he was going to walk into live electrical wiring since they were often pitch-black. After long days on the street, he went back to the single room he rents, where he took a long bath with Epsom salts, ate a mug of oatmeal with milk and sugar, watched TV, then went to sleep. He sometimes caught the end of a variety show, but mostly it was just the Spanish news. Joaquín fell asleep to news of the hurricane's damage. He didn't think of himself as a protagonist in the story of Sandy—he still doesn't—but he tells me his clearest memory of the hurricane aftermath is meeting two elderly Asian women so frail they could not carry anything and had nowhere to sleep. He gave them inflatable beds. It is one of the most prized memories of his life.

Julián volunteered, too. He fondly remembers traveling all across Staten Island and sometimes to New Jersey to go knocking door-to-door to see who needed help. He admits he felt sad that after the recovery efforts were well under way, the island forgot about the day laborers. He sometimes feels used, but he doesn't resent his neighbors and doesn't regret the time he spent helping them. "I was scared, there was disaster as far as the eye could see, I had friends who didn't make it, people got sick, but we helped each other out. We felt like we were part of the community. We finally felt like we belonged," he says.

One morning, outside a worker center, some day laborers came to me to talk about why I was there. *To write about them in a way they'd never been written about before!* I say. They had an ask. Could I please tell the real story about them? Not the one we're used to seeing in the papers, about them pissing in bottles and catcalling women. The real one. *Yes, yes,* I promise. I always promise things before I know whether or not I can deliver.

Some many months later I stumbled upon the story of Ubaldo Cruz Martinez. Ubaldo was an alcoholic and many of the day laborers I talked to knew him or knew of him but didn't really want to talk about him. They were so careful about their reputations and he was a homeless alcoholic who drowned in a basement during Hurricane Sandy because he was probably drunk. Did they feel sorry for him? Yes. Were they embarrassed by him? Probably.

Ubaldo was found floating in dirty water, and his body was

repatriated to his hometown of San Jerónimo Xayacatlán. The bell at the church rang at one o'clock in the morning to mark the return of one of their own. People in the town gossiped that it was a shame he had died with no friends and with nobody to cry over his grave.

Before the hour of this death, on October 31, Ubaldo leaned against a cement building for balance and he saw a small crescent of fur on the gravel, the rain already beating down. He walked to it, and discovered a small skinny squirrel, making a copper wiry sound, a wound on its abdomen. A stray, a stray like him. It was beginning to rain at a blunt slant, a lancing rain. He picked up the squirrel and walked into the basement where he was squatting. He made himself a Nescafé to sober up. The squirrel was cold to the touch so he put her in a shoe box and padded the box with his socks that he warmed in the oven. He had some condensed milk in the cupboard that he warmed in the microwave. He didn't have a dropper, so he fed it to her through a straw, sucking up the milk with his mouth, then putting his finger on the top of the straw, putting the straw into the squirrel's mouth, between her bunny teeth, to release the milk drop by drop. He knew he was not leaving this basement tonight. He couldn't get himself anywhere. No one would want him. They'd given up on him long ago. He had kids in Mexico. They'd be orphans. His heart raced. His hands became moist. Stroking the squirrel kept him calm as the basement filled with water. He put on his Ochoa jersey and a thin gold chain, and he decided to wait for what would come. He stroked the squirrel until the water got up to his shoulders and he treaded water. He held onto the shoe box above his head. No creature should have to die alone.

♦ ♦ ♦

Did this happen?

Are we in gangs?

Do we steal Social Security numbers?

Do we traffic our own children across the border?

Is this book nonfiction?

Can we imagine that he was capable of kindness, even as he was drinking? That he was capable of courage, even as he was wounded?

What if this is how, in the face of so much sacrilege and slander, we reclaim our dead?

CHAPTER 2

———— ⸰⸱⸰ ————

Ground Zero

On the morning of September 11, 2001, after the North Tower of the World Trade Center fell, killing some fourteen hundred people, firefighters rushed to the site with blueprints and floor plans, marking locations where they believed elevators and stairwells would have collapsed with the people they carried. They were looking for survivors. Global positioning technology plotted patterns formed by the spots where bodies, or parts of bodies, were found. But days went by and only eleven people were found in the rubble, and it soon became clear that the mapping technology would be used to locate the dead.

The fires at Ground Zero were mean and hard to extinguish; they burned long and deep, flaring when exposed to oxygen and fueled by tons of highly conductive papers and furniture soaked in jet fuel. Thermal heat maps from NASA and the U.S. Geological Survey showed swaths of rubble burning at temperatures above 1,292°F, hotter than the burning point of aluminum. By December 3, 2001, *New Scientist* dubbed it "the longest-burning structural fire in history." Officials continued to call Ground Zero a "rescue operation"—implying it was still possible to find survivors, but they couldn't keep hope alive and at the same time submerge all sixteen acres with water and flame retardant—until the hundredth day of the fire, when the last flame was extinguished.

Rescue workers called the sixteen acres of debris on Ground Zero "the Pile." The powdered debris in the Pile contained more than 150 compounds and elements including plaster, talc, synthetic foam, glass, paint chips, charred wood, slag wool, two hundred thousand pounds of lead from fifty thousand computers, gold and mercury from five hundred thousand fluorescent lights, two thousand tons of asbestos, and ninety-one thousand liters of jet fuel. The nearly three thousand human beings who died made up such a minuscule part of the debris that the odds of finding identifiable remains were less than one in a quadrillion. It was a site of desolation set on fire.

The first responders were firemen and EMT workers.

The second responders were undocumented immigrants.

Lucero Gómez is a social worker who runs informal group therapy sessions with mostly undocumented, all-Latinx former Ground Zero cleanup workers. Lucero tells me that almost immediately after 9/11, undocumented immigrants started getting phone calls "from a very underground kind of network of people who are undocumented and need work. They called at night. They said, 'Tomorrow there is work, come work.'" The city hired contractors—Americans, Anglo, white. The contractors hired subcontractors, many of them bilingual Latinx people with the golden ticket of American citizenship who could present themselves as friendly faces to other immigrants—"We look like you! We speak like you!"—and would make the eventual abuses unexpected. Vans drove from Queens out to Long Island, through Nassau and Suffolk Counties, up and down the immigrant enclaves, looking for day laborers to bring to Ground Zero. The workers were mostly Eastern European and Latin American. Many of the women knew the area well, having cleaned offices and apartments in Lower Manhattan for years. They knew they'd be called to dust. There was so much dust.

In 2001, Milton Vallejo had been working nights as a security guard at the World Trade Center. Milton is tall and gentle. On the morning of September 11, the day shift guards, friends of his, came in to take over and he joked around with them for a bit, then headed to the subway. He was underground when the news hit. He couldn't breathe. He raced home. He watched the news. He prayed to god. He had to help. It was his duty. Plus, work was work. The next day, he made his way back to the World Trade Center, now called Ground Zero. He found long lines of people waiting to enter the site. He wondered if he'd be asked to present his papers—the terrorists had been foreigners— and got out of line. An official of some kind—from where, he doesn't remember—overseeing the line walked over and asked him why he left the line. Milton fumbled. The truth is, I'm not here legally, he said. Get back in line, she said. When it was his turn, she had him sign his name on a blank sheet of paper and compared his signature to the signature on his Colombian passport. "They made all of us sign on blank paper, then compared the signature to any ID we had. Then they let us in," he says. At first, observers applauded them as they watched them work.

They took pictures. Then as the site began to crowd with cleanup workers, it was clear that most of them were Latinx. Some of the people observing them now started yelling, "Leave! Leave! Leave!"

"It looked like a Western, just like a desert," Milton says. "Everything was dust and water and there was no light any-where." Milton was assigned to clean basements, where he waded waist-deep through dirty water and chemicals. He tied plastic grocery bags around his ankles. The dust was the hard-est to clean because it blinded him and stuck to his wet cloth-ing. He wasn't given goggles. The subcontractors gave him air masks, but they were flimsy and broke easily. After a few days of work, Milton started spitting out mucus. Something scratched at the back of his throat, so he had to keep clearing it—something wet and dry at the same time. After one week, he got his first paycheck from the subcontractor: sixty dollars a day for work-ing a twelve-hour shift; some days were longer than twelve hours. When he tried cashing the check, it bounced.

I first met Milton at one of Lucero's group sessions in 2011. That day, the meeting was dedicated to a discussion of the September 11th Victim Compensation Fund and the James Zadroga 9/11 Health and Compensation Act, a law that promised to pro-vide medical treatment to 9/11 cleanup workers.

The people at Lucero's sessions had all become sick. They carry hospital ID cards issued by Mount Sinai and Bellevue, where they are treated. Many of them have developed cancer. They have rhinitis, gastritis, arthritis, severe acid reflux, asthma, high blood pressure, and back pain. They have PTSD, anxiety, depression, and paranoia. Their psychological symptoms are triggered by the smell of barbecue, by darkness, by any news coverage of natural disasters. The group helps them in some ways, but Lucero is just one person and cannot do it alone. Meetings are irregular.

When I return to visit the group again in early 2017, all anyone can talk about is deportation. A woman named Lourdes with two long braids reminds the group to be careful. She tells them to carry around their prescription bottles with them as well as their hospital ID cards to present to ICE officers should they be approached. She says ICE once entered her home but they left her alone once she was able to prove that she was receiving treatment at a local hospital's World Trade Center worker program. But that was one nice ICE officer, she says. Any of them could be deported at any time.

Lucero doesn't have much control over the group, which is rowdy. Everyone talks over one another and they sometimes answer their phones, screaming into them, while they're still in their seats. One man, Enrique, is quiet for most of the meeting. He tells me that nothing happened to him that day, that he was spared. He is wearing a light windbreaker that he leaves open, and he repeatedly brings one side of the jacket close to his face to take a sip from a straw. A bottle, in a brown paper bag, is in the inside pocket.

Enrique says he doesn't feel the effects of the cleanup, but it isn't true. He has flashbacks to Ground Zero all the time. A few weeks ago, he was working on top of a six-foot ladder in Brooklyn and had a flashback to being surrounded by dank water, in the dark, next to fallen lights, shattered glass, and ash, the strong smell of mildew and chemicals soaking fabrics and furniture. He fell off the ladder and broke his arm. "I become suddenly frightened by absolutely nothing, like a cat," he says.

Enrique was hired to work at Ground Zero by a company named Good Shine Cleaning, owned by a married Colombian American couple. American citizens. "The lines for cleaning jobs were hundreds of people long and companies just picked everyone up and put us in trucks," he remembers. "The Americans who own the contracting companies are all white. They hire Hispanic people to work as subcontractors and they're the ones who deal directly with laborers. When the American contractors come to the work sites, the subcontractors treat them like gods," he says. "They make us stop talking if we were talking, and we have to turn off the music if we were listening to music. We even stop working out of respect for them. They arrive in fancy cars and expensive clothes, and when they come in, they don't talk to us. They don't even look at us. They only talk to the Hispanic subcontractor." Contractors have mastered a plantation model in their line of work, exploiting whatever sense of community that might exist among Latinx people. The workers think there are people along the chain of command who are watching out for them, but melanin and accents are ineffective binding substances.

I know the members of the therapy group struggle with mental illness, and when I ask, gently, what meds they're on or what their panic attacks are like, they tell me but seem a little embarrassed. In our community, there is an ingrained idea that if you are sick, it's a weakness, a symptom of our internalized bootstraps mythology. "You don't have to pretend with me," I say. We end up confiding in each other.

Milton attends the 9/11 group therapy meetings regularly, and when he sees me again, after so many years, he bows slightly, kisses my hand, and says, "Señorita Karla, you've returned." He is on medication now, and it has helped, but at the beginning of his treatment, things were bad. "I tried to take my life," he says. A psychologist who worked with some of the 9/11 survivors talked him down from overdosing on pills over the phone, reassuring him that he was loved. Milton also sees a psychiatrist who once talked him down from throwing himself onto the train tracks.

Milton speaks in an overly formal way with the affect of a dictator. This makes me think of my father, another amateur Fidel—and I think about meeting my father for what felt like the first time, all those years ago, when I was five. One of the first things he did was take me to the zoo. It was both random and perfect, a reminder that we were still here, animals ourselves, on earth.

I ask Milton if he'd like to go to the Queens Zoo. He says yes.

The Queens Zoo does not have a lion, which is the mascot of Milton's favorite soccer team. Milton used to play professionally in Colombia, and then he played in a league of immigrant men every week in the park for years, before he was diagnosed with asthma after 9/11 and had to stop. Although he has mixed feelings about observing animals that are "trapped," Milton takes lots of pictures at the zoo. He has never been to one before, and I wish I had taken him to the Bronx Zoo, which is bigger and better in every way. The only animals here are coyotes, elk, owls, pumas, lynx, bald eagles, cranes, alligators (seasonal), bison, antelope, peccaries, thick-billed parrots, and Andean bears. It is cold and windy, not a great day to spend time outdoors, and Milton is wearing a cream coat over a white puff vest, white sneakers, and a checkered gray scarf. I'm wearing a puff coat too, and sometimes when we pass our reflections on the glass panes of animal exhibits, I wonder whether a stranger passing us would think I am his daughter.

We go by the graveyard of extinct animals. It is what it sounds like—tombstones on the ground with pictures of extinct species and their year of extinction. There is a golden toad (1989), a dodo bird (1681), a Tasmanian tiger (1936), and pig-footed bandicoot (1901). Do you know what that is? When they were alive, they looked like tiny sand-colored mice with bunny ears, and stood with a kangaroo's stance—really cute. Milton feels genuinely sad that these animals are gone and tells me he hates the American culture of hunting. "Hunting for pleasure is putting an end to creation. God creates for a reason," he says.

Does god allow death for a reason? I ask him. Milton does not know.

The chief tragedy in Milton's life is the loss of his friend Rafael Hernández, a Mexican volunteer firefighter who also served as a 9/11 first responder. Milton met Rafael at a resting station for relief workers, where he saw him in a blue helmet. "It looked like he was wearing a costume," he says. He asked Rafael if he spoke Spanish. "Uh, I'm Mexican," Rafael replied. They became friends.

Rafael had been a firefighter in Mexico and showed his Mexican firefighter badge to the first responders, and they geared him up. They didn't care that he was foreign. They needed all the help they could get. As everyone else was running out of the buildings, Rafael ran up the North Tower. He encountered a pregnant woman whose water broke. She begged him not to leave her, and he didn't. He reportedly carried her down twenty-eight flights of stairs. Not long after they made it out, the tower fell.

Rafael didn't leave Ground Zero for months, working day after day. Eventually his lungs got so fucked up he had to be hooked up to a respirator to sleep. He died in 2011, the ten-year anniversary of 9/11. Milton shows me a shrink-wrapped CD a folksinger friend had made in honor of the anniversary. The back of the CD shows a fading image of the two towers with the faces of Milton and Rafael above them. Rafael was declared to have died of "natural causes," which officials later explained actually meant "alcoholism and obesity," but Latinx leaders in New York have refused to accept that pronouncement. His body was repatriated to Mexico and his organs kept in New York for further investigation. In a Fox News Latino television interview taped before his death, Rafael is incorrectly introduced as "Juan Hernandez: Hero in His Adopted Homeland." The camera zooms in on his heavily inked upper arm, tattooed with a huge bald eagle, an American flag, the downtown Manhattan skyline, the Twin Towers, and his initials: "R. H. Mex."

Their friendship was so famous that some gossips in Queens say they were gay, Milton tells me. He misses Rafael. He was the only person who could really understand what it was like to be there. As a way of coping, Milton has written a memoir called *Sueño, pesadilla, paraíso* ("Dream, Nightmare, Paradise"). He explains the title: "My dream was never money. I had a great job in Colombia. My ex-wife and I fled the war. Before Pablo Escobar was extradited, he ordered bombs to be planted everywhere as an act of revenge, and I narrowly escaped two bombs—a car bomb and a bomb at a local mall. So my dream was to find a peaceful life. My nightmare was 9/11, and also going from working in an office to being mistreated in a factory—to being treated like an uneducated person. My paradise is having found god, and paradise will be returning to Colombia when I am old." After he told Rafael he was writing a book, his friend used to say he wanted to weld together their living room walls, his in Mexico and Milton's in Colombia, so they could share a wall and write their books together as old men.

Milton believes that he has been chosen by god to be a messenger for the Ground Zero undocumented workers, maybe for our people in general. He looks so damn earnest when he says this—not in the pathetic way that makes me want to kill myself, in the self-assured way that makes me feel like I'm back in my mother's uterus—that I almost believe him. When I mention this to my friends, they think it's fanaticism, but I don't. I believe him.

The first of our losses happened on September 11, 2001. Years later, during my freshman year at college, a popular topic of conversation in the dining hall was where you were on 9/11. I learned that no matter how far away you were from New York that day, no matter how distant your connection to that day was, no matter how much lower than zero the count of the people you lost on that day was, if you were white, 9/11 happened to you personally, with blunt and scalding force. Because the antithesis of an American is an immigrant and because we could not be victims in the public eye, we became suspects. And so September 11 changed the immigration landscape forever. Muslims and Sikhs became the target of hate crimes. ICE was the creation of 9/11 paranoia. The Secure Communities program would require local police to share information with Homeland Security. Immigration detention centers began to be managed by private prison groups. And New York State, as well as most other states, axed driver's licenses for undocumented immigrants.

I think about this often; that was the night my dad started dying. In this memory, my father comes home from work and I greet him in the doorway to give him a kiss hello and ask for his blessing. Do you know this custom? I've only seen Ecuadorians do it. You go up to your elders and say "Bendición," and they kiss you or do the sign of the cross on your forehead and chest and say "Bendición." It's how you say hello or goodbye, like your de facto state is a state of cursedness and your elders can un- curse you, but only for a little while, so you have to keep asking. So I stand in the doorway in my bare feet and say "Hello, Father. Blessing please." He walks slowly and comes toward my body at a strange angle a child could only interpret as a terrible fall. He collapses onto me to cry into my neck. I'm little, but he does. Collapse, I mean. My father the dictator, heaving full-throated sobs. He hands me a letter. The letter says, in English, that Governor George Pataki had suspended driver's licenses for un- documented immigrants as part of a national security measure. My father had just lost his job as a taxi driver. He had also lost his state ID. Over the next two decades, he'd lose many more things, but let's put a little blue thumbtack on this memory map, the first place in hell we visited.

It was hard to see my father fall because he was the most powerful person I knew. He had kept me alive. He was a dif- ficult man and he had recognized me as a difficult child. I was polite and craved approval from authority figures, but I was also dark and precocious. Not precocious in the we-live-in- Tribeca-and-my-kid-is-a-born-artist kind of way. More like my

immigrant-third-grader-is-reading-Hemingway-but-is-secretly-
drinking-Listerine-and-toothpaste-until-she-throws-up-because-
she-wants-it-to-kill-her kind of way. My father read parenting
books about how to raise troubled children, but those children
were never straight-A students who were soft-spoken and loved
teachers. It confused him, and the dissonance made him angry
at me. When I was off from school, for any kind of break, my
father would plan out my day in half-hour increments, schedul-
ing everything from bath time to TV shows to coloring time
to math drills to time to play with dolls, and even bathroom
breaks. He called it my schedule and he handwrote it on graph
paper in different colored inks and taped it to my desk. My
mother stayed home at the time, and she enforced the schedule.
If I became too emotional, I was sent to take a cold shower. If
my mood became low, he made me go running or roller-skating.
He'd give me research projects about animals or important politicians and entire passages from the Bible to memorize. He'd
set aside magazine or newspaper articles for me to translate in
perfect handwriting into blank notebooks. He could not review
the fidelity of the translation but he judged my penmanship. I
don't know what would have happened to me if I had not been
kept away from my own thoughts for so many years. I believe
god sent my father. Maybe that's why I believe god could have
sent Milton, too.

Paloma is an older member of Lucero's support group. She
talks like a mumble rapper, low and guttural and with a deliber-
ate lack of enunciation. She can laugh and cry within seconds.
Paloma is recovering from cancer, lives alone, and is severely
traumatized. She says she is so afraid of ICE activity that she
literally runs in and out of doctors' appointments so they don't

catch her. Like, *runs*. She has installed surveillance cameras outside her apartment in case agents come to her door. "They don't
want us in this country," she says. "We have to be careful."

One Sunday I meet Paloma at the ten o'clock mass at Sacred
Heart of Jesus Church in Queens but she does not want me to
sit with her. "You can meet me outside after," she says. The
church is filled with a couple hundred families. I take a seat in
the back.

The Catholic Church is, above all things, reliable across centuries. I can see this same mass taking place at the height of the
Cold War, maybe even during the Inquisition. The priest has
white skin and white hair, while the hundreds in the pews are
brown-skinned people with black, black hair. He hates one
bishop. He loves another bishop. They're not even American
bishops. He sometimes makes side comments under his breath
that I assume he assumes the congregants won't catch ("Marga-
ret Thatcher, a British woman who looked like a man") during a
short rant against communism. He advises the congregants
against practicing witchcraft or seeking traditional healing
when they return to their home countries "on vacation," and
leads them in prayer, asking god "that the church be enriched
by mercy and charity" before passing the collection plate. It's
been a while since I've been to church, and I'd forgotten the
back rows are reserved for people who go in and out, mothers
with young babies. ("This is the scandalous symphony we've
been listening to all morning," the priest mutters harshly when
he hears the cries of a baby with Down syndrome being held by
a young woman standing in the aisle.) Today's reading is from
St. Paul's letter to the Ephesians. There is talk about abomina-
tions. I look up at the ceiling.

I meet Paloma outside, by a white marble statue of Jesus Christ yanking open his flowing robes, revealing his sacred heart. The sacred heart of Jesus is depicted as the literal coronary organ— pierced, aflame, surrounded by thorns, and wounded. It signifies the power of his love for us. I've seen it tattooed on gangsters and I love it.

We walk several blocks to La Hacienda, a Colombian restaurant that I remember loving as a child. On the way there, Paloma repeatedly walks into traffic. She doesn't look both ways, she doesn't even look one way, she just lunges in front of honking SUVs. I don't say anything but link my arm through hers to guide her, at times pulling her back so she's not hit by a car. Her vision is fine. I wonder if it's a death wish, Freud something something, but then I notice that I can't see more than a few feet ahead of me. Women roast corn and kebabs on makeshift grills on every corner, and cumbia blasts from record stores that still sell CDs. My senses feel rushed. It's a short walk to the restaurant, but Paloma gets short of breath and struggles to talk on account of her ruined lungs. I get out of breath, too.

At the restaurant, she orders raspberry juice in milk and I order a Corona. Whenever I steer the conversation to 9/11, she begins to cry. My parents scolded and taunted me whenever I cried as a child—they found it weak and threatening— and so I don't like to see people cry. It embarrasses and angers me. I change the topic every time her eyes water. Paloma had cleaned properties in Lower Manhattan that included international banks and—the irony—the former Immigration and Naturalization Service building. (INS became ICE in 2003.) On the morning of 9/11, she was working on the fortieth floor of a government building when a fire erupted in the elevator—

the buildings around the World Trade Center were also damaged by the blasts—and the workers had to flee down the stairs. She left a shoe behind. The building was still smoking when they returned to clean. "We even ate on top of the dust," she says. "Yes, we were heroes, but the dangers of the job were hidden from us so that we could work. If they had put up a sign at the site listing what we could come to face, we wouldn't have gone in."

Paloma has a string of illnesses that are common to all of the cleanup workers—sleep apnea, PTSD, depression, anxiety, gastrointestinal issues. She also has breast cancer. She can't work because her bones hurt, and she often gets fevers, chills, and vertigo. She is waiting for the Zadroga Act to send her a compensation check, which some friends have already received, *friends who don't even have cancer.*

Paloma fled Colombia for the usual reasons—economic depression, bankruptcy in the family, the need to support her ailing mother. But she also had another reason. "The truth is I am an escape artist," she says. Paloma grew up with an abusive stepfather. Once, after he beat her, she swore she would run away as soon as she had the chance. This was the 1970s in small-town Colombia, and she was a sixteen-year-old girl. Her only way to escape was to get married, so that's what she did— she married the first guy who asked. She was seventeen. "I did it to escape," she says. She immediately got pregnant, and would come to have three daughters. She didn't love being a mom but she did her best. She got increasingly restless as the years went by. It all began to change when her fifteen-year-old daughter Lucy got pregnant and her boyfriend didn't want to marry her. ("Am I supposed to marry her just to make you happy?" the boy yelled at Paloma. So she punched him in the face.) Lucy bounced back quickly after childbirth and began leaving the baby with Paloma all the time so she could go out with her boyfriend or go to parties. Paloma didn't love being a grandma, and she didn't love being a full-time babysitter. "I didn't want to live that life. I got tired of it. I'm not the type of woman who just puts up with shit," she tells me. "I wasn't born to be just a mother, just a grandmother, just a wife. So I escaped." She left her grand-child, her three daughters (including one who was just seven years old), and her husband, and she came to the United States alone.

Paloma tells me that her brother drowned himself, one of her cousins hanged himself, and another one threw himself off a tall building in Bogotá. She wonders: If she had stayed in Colombia, would she have followed suit? She acknowledges this thought with contempt. "What they did was cowardly," she says. "My entire family is weak. I'm not weak like them. I'd rather be mis-erable here than end up in a cemetery in Colombia. I'm here, and I may be crying, but at least I'm not dead." I ask Paloma if she would choose to have children if she had a second shot at life, and she thinks for a long time, wrapping her head around the fact that it could be a choice. "No," she says finally. She has spent years apologizing to her daughters, but they resent her for the abandonment and it's a wound that doesn't heal. It's what would await her in Colombia if she went back. More open wounds. After she finishes her juice, she leans close to me and tells me about Cruz.

Cruz is a little older than she is. Cuban. When he was young, he was bad, served his time, but he's clean now. They met when he was working delivering furniture and delivered a refrigerator to her home. He told her he liked her—a straight shooter, which she admired—and he gave her his phone number. Six months passed, and she called him one evening. "I was bored," she says, giggling. They went out for cappuccinos and talked all night. He wasn't scared by her baggage, by the depression and panic attacks, and she comforted him because he had been recently widowed. Cruz wants to marry Paloma, but she won't divorce her husband in Colombia, even though soon after she left, he began dating the children's teenage nanny, because when he dies she is entitled to part of his pension. She and the nanny will split it. I love this woman.

Paloma was diagnosed with breast cancer in 2010. Her doctors believe the cancer is linked to her elevated exposure to toxins during the post-9/11 cleanup work. The news made Paloma feel bitter, hopeless, and punished by god. Surely he was punishing her for abandoning her children. What kind of mother would do that? She threw herself into church, into prayer. She spends a lot of time online watching Christian movies and reading Christian blogs. "I'm more than a believer," she says. "I'm a fanatic. I see Jesus Christ right in front of me, as real as I see you."

At first, Cruz would accompany her to her doctors' appointments. After her surgery, he hid in the hospital room so he wouldn't be kicked out after visiting hours and could spend the night with her. But she was getting ready to die. She took all her savings, including a little compensation money she had received from the September 11th Victim Compensation Fund, and traveled to Panama alone. The first vacation of her life. Then she went back to Colombia, why else but to die, to die in her homeland surrounded by family, which seemed appropriate, even if she knew they wouldn't give her a hero's welcome, and they didn't. Then, at a routine doctor's appointment in Colombia, the doctor told her that she was cancer-free. "I said, I'm out of here!" she says, and she peaced out just like that. She came back to the United States by a means I am not going to disclose. She arrived in Las Vegas, and Cruz rented a truck from New York, driving for days to pick her up and bring her back to the city. On their road trip, they'd drive for seven-hour stretches, then stop at the closest town to explore. "It was a special trip," she says. "One of the most special moments of my life. Can you believe he did that?" At a routine appointment in New York, the doctor told her he had bad news. The cancer was back, and it was aggressive. After several rounds of chemotherapy, Paloma is too weak to work and her savings are depleted.

I ask for the check, and Paloma asks that both our leftovers— roast chicken, rice and beans, sweet plantain—be packed to go. I ask her if we can pass by a Colombian bakery so I can buy her some baked goods. "Sweetie, I would say yes, but I'm on a diet," she says. Her doctor told her she's a little on the heavy side for her height. She plans to lose twenty-five pounds. Tonight she will eat our leftovers. Tomorrow she will eat only apples. She walks me to my train stop, again veering into traffic unless I hold tightly on to her arm, the fog thick and close to the ground so we can't see ahead of us and we can't see our feet. When I hug her, I slip a twenty-dollar bill into her hand. "For a special treat," I tell her. "I'm on a diet, Karlita, but god bless you," she says.

Like Paloma, some of the members of Lucero's group have already received a few thousand dollars here and there through the September 11th Victim Compensation Fund, a program set

aside by the federal government for proven victims of the attacks and their living relatives. The man in charge of evaluating
applications for the fund was Kenneth R. Feinberg, a lawyer
who had successfully settled the Agent Orange lawsuits on be-
half of the U.S. government. He had unlimited funds but a clear
end date. In 2003, the fund stopped accepting applications, a
time when many individuals were only beginning to exhibit
symptoms. Workers who did not make the deadline fell back on
unsubsidized treatment in city hospitals or workers' compensation payments. Treatment options were slim for undocumented
immigrants.

Over the phone, Feinberg tells me he thought that the 9/11
Fund was "an extraordinary example of inclusiveness."

"At the urging of Attorney General John Ashcroft, we pro-
mulgated that no immigrant in the country illegally would be
harmed, we translated the application and rules into four languages including Spanish, Korean, maybe French. We made
sure that all immigrants were given the opportunity for free
legal counsel. We held town hall meetings in the Bronx where
we explained to surviving immigrants that the death of their
husbands would in no way prevent them from filing." He laughs.
"I can't think of a federal program more inclusive and respectful
of diversity."

But in order for victims to be recognized by the Victim Compensation Fund, they had to show paperwork proving they
worked at Ground Zero or lost someone that day. The undocumented often work in clever ways to leave no paper trail. There
is no telling how many were killed because restaurant owners
and managers have refused to come forward with the names of
missing people for fear that they will be fined for employing

undocumented laborers. Deliverymen lost their brothers that day. Some men worked the "graveyard shift"—between midnight and 8:00 A.M.—and were finishing up their last deliveries and going home when the planes struck. Advocacy organizations like Asociación Tepeyac worked tirelessly to field calls from families who had not heard from a loved one, and later to help the men and women who cleaned up Ground Zero. Dr. Charles Hirsch, New York City's chief medical examiner, became "the gatekeeper to the official list" of WTC victims. The final list contained 2,749 names of deaths that had been ruled homicides. These 2,749 names would be inscribed on the memorial. The chief medical examiner's office said that there were no more missing people. Said Julie Bolcer, director of public affairs, "The list accounts for everyone known or reported to have been there. There are no unknowns." A few weeks after the towers fell, the city gave families who reported disappearances an urn containing Ground Zero ashes. The Mexican consulate held its own memorial service, reading the names we know and praying for the names we don't.

After my father lost his job as a taxi driver, he found a job as a deliveryman at a restaurant down in the Financial District. Deliverymen in that area call themselves "delivery boys." Throughout my teens, I always corrected my father when he said this because I assumed the guys had heard it from some white supremacist boss who was trying to emasculate them and they accepted it as a neutral term. It made me furious. "There's a history to white people calling men of color boys," I would tell him.

In the mornings, my father would deliver breakfast to offices in the Financial District. A raisin bagel with cream cheese and

coffee with hazelnut creamer. A blueberry muffin and black coffee; two cranberry scones and three coffees, two cream, one
sugar. A single croissant, and a single coffee, sent back because
it was brought with white sugar and not Splenda. Bacon, egg,
and cheese sandwiches. Oatmeal with brown sugar. Yogurt par-
faits. Orange juice and a banana. A chamomile tea. A granola
bar and a chocolate milk. There was no delivery minimum, so
my father delivered it all. Because the deliveries were so small,
sometimes he didn't get a tip. Sometimes he was told to keep the
change—a quarter. Sometimes he was tipped in pennies. He had
to say, "Thank you, sir. Thank you, ma'am." Sometimes he was
given a twenty-dollar tip for a five-dollar breakfast. He always
told us about those tips. They were usually from Puerto Rican
executive assistants who talked to him in Spanish and asked to
see photos of me, so good and studious, bangs cut right above
my eyebrows. My father complimented their nails and asked to
see photos of their babies.

Sometimes the deliverymen carried catering orders. Those
would sometimes involve two deliverymen, but that wasn't
ideal because they had to split the tip. You never wanted to split
the tip. The delivery orders were large, but you can carry a lot
with two hands if you really try. The breakfast catering orders
were usually an assortment of scones, croissants, muffins, and
bagels. You couldn't eat one yourself, though. The boss always
knew if you ate one. If you needed a water, you had to go up to
the cash register and buy the water. There was no discount.
Sometimes the older men needed a Red Bull, but the boss put up
security cameras in the kitchen area so he could tell if you had a
Red Bull. He wouldn't even charge you for it if you had one.
He'd just fire you. Do you think I need you? I don't even need to

put an ad in the newspaper for this job. There are twenty Mexicans who'd line up for your job—you think I'm going to spot you a Red Bull?

My father is an aesthete. Everyone wanted him for the catering orders because he'd do beautiful designs with the scones and the muffins. Like topiary shit. He sometimes had to write labels on heavy stock printer paper and he'd use his fanciest script; he taught himself calligraphy, like he taught himself everything, and everyone would go, Wow, you're so talented! They always made him write the words on cakes. Beautiful fucking handwriting. He'd come home glowing if they complimented his handwriting. (My cursive was beautiful for a long time until I started taking lithium and then my hand shook bad. My dad was so sad.)

My father didn't use a bike; he made all his deliveries on foot. He speed-walked while carrying many heavy bags of food to offices on Wall Street. The plastic handles of the bags would twist and cut into his fingers, and he eventually developed large calluses on both his hands. His polyester pants rubbed up against his calves so much that he eventually lost all the hair on his legs. They're smooth as a baby's bottom, even now. He went through many pairs of inexpensive black rubber shoes. My mother massaged his feet at night. My dad's feet are small and fat, like mine, so you can't tell when they're swollen. After a few years, my dad's feet would hurt so much that he walked like he was on hot coals, sometimes leaning on me to move from the couch to the bed. "Ay ay ay ay," he'd say as he limped, like a mariachi. Most of my dad's co-workers were Mexican, and he learned how to cook Mexican food from them and he learned Mexican swear words, which my mom hated. Some of them were young, teenagers, and

my dad would scold them and tell them to go back to school. He
made his first gay friend at that restaurant. They called him
Che, because he was Argentine.

When I was in high school, my dad began to share stories
he'd heard about undocumented restaurant workers who'd died
on 9/11. I decided to interview my dad's co-workers for the
first piece I had ever pitched, for *The Tribeca Trib*. They were
the only other undocumented people I knew. I had just watched
All the President's Men and wanted to break a story.

My father picked whom I could talk to, and he chaperoned
the interviews. He bought me a yellow flip notebook because I
was pretending to be a journalist and he knew that would make
me feel important. He also bought me a tape recorder from
Kmart. I never actually managed to talk to anyone who directly
knew an undocumented restaurant worker who died on 9/11,
but everyone had heard the stories.

The undocumented immigrants who died on 9/11 worked in
restaurants, in housekeeping, in security. They were also deliverymen. The 9/11 Memorial and Museum now stands where
the Twin Towers once stood. They have an exhibit that gutted
me when I saw it. It's a bicycle, presumed to have belonged to a
deliveryman, a bike that was left tied to a pole near the Twin
Towers. Visitors to the site had left acrylic flowers—red, white,
and blue roses and carnations. They also left a rosary on the
bicycle. It became a makeshift memorial. There was a note on
the street next to the bike. EN MEMORIA DE LOS DELIVERY BOYS QUE
MURIERON. SEPT 11 2001. "In memory of the delivery boys who
died." Delivery boys. That's how I know it was the delivery
boys who put up that sign, who left those acrylic flowers, men
like my dad.

I wonder what the bike owner brought to the Twin Towers that day. It was September, a mild day, so maybe an iced coffee. Black. Probably a scone. Maybe a $4.50 breakfast. A 15 percent tip would be sixty-seven cents. A 20 percent tip would be ninety cents. A generous person might tip a dollar. My father would travel anywhere for a dollar. My father would chase a dollar down the road, a dollar blowing in the winds of a hurricane, even when there was an equal likelihood of getting swept up by the wind. My dad would always take the chance. A dollar is a dollar.

There was Antonio Meléndez, and Antonio Javier Álvarez, and Leobardo López Pascual, and Juan Ortega-Campos, and Martín Morales Zempoaltécatl, and Arturo Alba Moreno, and José Manuel Contreras Fernández, and Germán Castillo García, and José Guevara González, and Alicia Acevedo Carranza, and Víctor Antonio Martínez Pastrana, and Juan Romero Orozco, and Enrique Octavio and Santos Anaya, and Margarito Casillas, and Norberto Hernández.

There was also Fernando Jimenez Molinar, who worked at a pizza shop nearby, delivering pies and washing dishes. He was nineteen years old. (My brother is nineteen years old. Jesus Christ, the hair above my brother's lip, he's so proud of it that he doesn't shave. He writes spoken-word poetry and keeps a dream journal. I bought it for him; it has Batman on the cover. He collects comic books.) Fernando had two roommates, undocumented like him, and they called his mom when he didn't come home on the night of 9/11. A local Mexican organization looked everywhere for him. He was gone. The Twin Towers fell shortly before 10:00 A.M. Who wanted a pizza delivered that early? Probably a finance bro coked up after a long night lying with numbers. Maybe he was high on Adderall. Hadn't eaten in twenty-four hours and was finally hungry, but only for pizza. Probably a little older than Fernando, maybe twenty-two or twenty-three. Harvard grad. Bro, is that my pizza?

Fernando's mom didn't want him to come to America. He went anyway. He grew out his hair into a ponytail and grew a beard. That's what the newspapers say. But he was nineteen, and I know nineteen. Nice beard. His sneakers were clean, white, like a fool's. My father always told his teenage co-workers not to get white sneakers, and they always did anyway. Slaves to fashion. Earbuds in his ears. Metallica. Mexicans and their Metallica. It's not racist when I say it. It was bright and sunny that day. His life ahead of him. The day ahead of him. His mom still young. He could still change her life. He could still tell his father off. The pizza delivery would net him five dollars. That's a calling card. He could call his mom, but the entire card would be spent on her sending him blessings. He wanted to buy her a house. A garden where she could grow her own flowers; she loved mari- golds, not bodega flowers like rainbow-colored carnations— marigolds. The house would have one room for her, and an office where she could read her Bible. The edges of the pages were colored gold. He would get his mom a dog so she wouldn't be lonely. She liked frilly things, so maybe she'd like a poodle, but he wanted to get her a German shepherd, something to pro- tect her, bark if anyone but him approached the house. So many people had hurt his mother, but not again. Not under his watch. His mother, his saint. Sometimes he'd swing by hair salons and steal the lady magazines and send them to her. Sometimes when he called she'd describe the dresses she loved from the maga- zines over the phone, and he resolved to buy them. She loved silk. His mother never knew silk. He'd make her know silk. He'd make her know death. He'd make her know silence. He'd make her know the death mask of a man disappeared, incinerated, and gone. Fernando Jimenez Molinar? Was he ever alive?

Did you know that before dialing Mexico you have to dial 011? There are so many numbers to dial to get to your mother. 1 2 3 4 5 6 7 8 9 0. You learn those numbers young. The jet-fuel smell thick in the air, the flame and smoke surrounding you, you can only get to 011 and that's enough to make you foreign, to make you other, to make you Mexican. You take out your wallet and put an ID between your teeth so they can find you when it all collapses. Your flesh may burn but your teeth will remain and the ID will be there. It's a fake ID. Nobody will ever know you died. Nobody will ever know you lived.

CHAPTER 3

Miami

The city of Hialeah in Miami-Dade County is the last bit of U.S. soil on which Amelia Earhart stood before embarking on her doomed solo flight in 1937, disappearing in the Pacific Ocean somewhere near Howland Island. I'm about to go to Hialeah on a reporting trip, so I text this factoid to my mother. At fifty-three, she is in the middle of a feminist awakening and is usually eager to talk about feminist heroes to compare herself to—unlike my father, who compares me to those women instead. A few days later, she texts me a picture of a tiny pilot costume for a dog, saying she is at a white people's pet boutique and she is about to buy my dog, Frankie, a leather jacket and matching pilot cap. Oh my god, I say.

I never write about my mother. *Why do you never write about me?* my mother asks, a copy of *The New York Times* on her lap open to a two-page spread about my father. *Of course I write about you,* I say. *You don't,* she says. I don't, it's true I don't. The obvious answer to that is that I have daddy issues. ("Stop saying that," my partner says. "It doesn't mean what you think it means.") My father was the one who worked outside the house for twenty-five years, so he was the one facing grueling labor conditions and racist abuse on the front lines in America. I thought my mother was protected somehow because she was in the home.

And when she stepped out into the wild to work outside the home three years ago, she went to work for these white people who didn't abuse her so I was like, okay, we're *okay*. Working outside the home changed her, she became this whole new woman, emancipated and bold, and it caused problems at home. *You always take your father's side*, she said, *adiós*. She was always hanging up on me. *I am not taking my father's side! I'm being objective!* I scream into the phone, but she's gone. She drinks organic kombucha, once mailed me a leather leash because she thought Frankie looked "homeless," and has zero tolerance for my father's temper, the third member of their marriage.

I sometimes fantasize about my parents divorcing. It'd devastate my brother but that's why I pay for his therapy. I'd be relieved. I've looked for houses in Havana where my dad wants to "retire" and I can maybe afford that, if I sell a book and TV show every few years, and keep my kidneys healthy and available. I imagine my mom would live with my brother, who will remain a Jehovah's Witness, like our parents, and marry someone young and nice and equally interested in having two biological children. My brother sure does love my mother, in a whole, pure, white-woman-at-a-farmer's-market kind of way, but that's because my mom didn't leave him in Ecuador before he could speak, so there aren't many things unsaid between them.

I've always been super casual when people ask me about my parents having left me in Ecuador. That's a bravado I'd like to keep on the official record but something else intrudes. I love my mom. She's a hard worker. She's a feminist. She's kind to you if you're 1) my partner or 2) a formerly abused dog. But we haven't talked about her leaving me in Ecuador when I was a year and a half old. Sometimes I do adorable things like take pictures of myself chugging vodka bottles or pretending to down the contents of a pill bottle and send them to her with the caption "because you abandoned me" but, lately, in response to those jokes, she's begun to suggest it was my dad's fault. When I meet a toddler, I'm like, damn, I was a *baby* baby. When I am away from my partner and dog for a few days for work, and it's hard, I wonder how they were able to do it for five years.

I don't blame either of them for it. I never have. What I'm describing to you is dirt extracted from a very tight pore. I don't feel anything about being left on the day-to-day but I am told by mental health experts that it has affected me. And I fought that conclusion. I denied it. I wanted to be a genius. I wanted my mental illnesses to be purely biological. I wanted to have been born wild and crazy and weird and brilliant, writing math equations in chalk on a window. Instead, therapist after therapist told me I had attachment issues and that my mental illnesses were related to my childhood. I left those therapists. Ghosted them.

But it's not just those early years without my parents that branded me. It's the life I've led in America as a migrant, watching my parents pursue their dream in this country and then having to deal with its carcass, witnessing the crimes against migrants carried out by the U.S. government with my hands bound. As an undocumented person, I felt like a hologram. Nothing felt secure. I never felt safe. I didn't allow myself to feel joy because I was scared to attach myself to anything I'd have to let go of. Being deportable means you have to be ready to go at any moment, ready to go with nothing but the clothes on your body. I've learned to develop no relationship to anything, not to photos, not to people, not to jewelry or clothing or ticket stubs or stuffed animals from childhood. Sometimes to prove my ability to let go, I'll write something long and delete it, or go on my phone and delete all the photos I have of happy memories. I've never loved a material object. When my parents took me home after my Harvard graduation, we took the Chinatown bus, and we each took one suitcase. If it didn't fit, we threw it out. We threw out everything that wasn't clothes.

The U.S. government's crimes against immigrants are beyond the pale and the whole world knows. At protests I've been to outside of courthouses and ICE offices, I've seen white people carry signs plastered with images of the drowned bodies of Oscar Alberto Martinez Ramirez and his toddler, Angie Valeria, on the banks of the Rio Grande. But when I was growing up, and throughout the Obama administration, these same crimes were happening, if on a different scale, and I'm not sure the same people cared. I felt crazy for thinking we were under attack, watching my neighbors disappear and then going to school and watching the nightly news and watching award shows and seeing no mention. I felt crazy watching the white supremacist state slowly kill my father and break my family apart. I would frantically tell everyone that there was no such thing as the American Dream but then some all-star immigrants around me who had done things "the right way" preached a different story and Americans ate that up. It all made me feel crazy. I also am crazy. Pero why? My diagnoses are borderline personality disorder, major depression, anxiety, and OCD. (I love diagnoses. Gives you the ability to read about yourself.) Researchers have shown that the flooding of stress hormones resulting from a traumatic separation from your parents at a young age kills off so many dendrites and neurons in the brain that it results in permanent psychological and physical changes. One psychiatrist I went to told me that my brain looked like a tree without branches.

So I just think about all the children who have been separated from their parents, and there's a lot of us, past and present, and some under more traumatic circumstances than others—like those who are in internment camps right now—and I just imagine us as an army of mutants. We've all been touched by this monster, and our brains are forever changed, and we all have trees without branches in there, and what will happen to us? Who will we become? Who will take care of us?

I went to Miami in 2017, shortly after the House of Representatives voted 217 to 213 to replace the Affordable Care Act with a new piece of legislation that listed cesarean sections, rape, and depression as preexisting conditions. Experts estimated it would strip healthcare from twenty-three million Americans over the next decade. Miami could hardly afford the blow. Miami-Dade has the state's largest number of employed yet uninsured adults, as well as record-setting rates of heart disease, diabetes, and HIV infection.

Undocumented immigrants in Florida who do not have insurance have experiences that are not dissimilar from those of other uninsured people, but the key difference is that it is impossible for undocumented immigrants to purchase insurance, even if they can afford it. One of the bogeymen of the right, in this country or any Western country, is the image of the sick immigrant—the supposed strain on the healthcare system, the burden on emergency rooms and taxpayers. I cannot overstate how little interest I have in changing the minds of people who might believe this—I'd honestly rather swallow a razor blade than be expected to change the mind of a xenophobe. But I'm curious about the bogeyman so I thought to explore it.

What I discovered was a story about illness and healing in migrant communities through the lens of women—caretakers and rebels. These women were also coincidentally like my mother, immigrant women married to immigrant men, mothers to immigrant and citizen children, looking back on decades of the American Dream and taking stock.

During my first trip, they were kind, nurturing, supportive, and so proud of me. We kept in touch all year. I'm ashamed to say it, but I sometimes fantasized about one of them being my mom. *You're so beautiful and so smart!* they'd text me with a flurry of heart emojis, and I'd compare that to my mother sending me pictures of herself in mink hats and vintage dresses, saying I needed to lose thirty pounds before her death so I could inherit her clothing. But when I visited the ladies in Miami a second time, a year later, they sounded more like my mom. They confided in me the same things she has confided in me. They were restless. They wanted more for their lives, and I couldn't help them.

♦ ♦ ♦

Julieta and I meet at the corner of a construction site. The air is thick with dust, and against the grim heat and among the empty storefront windows stands a small coral building with a roof painted gold. A placard outside advertises Macondo, the local pharmacy.

Julieta is thirty-nine years old and Nicaraguan, a big woman with the cheerful, paranoid manner of a debutante with a secret. The morning we see each other, she has her hair in a messy knot and is on her way to the beauty salon to get ready for her goddaughter's quinceañera. She doesn't talk about her children unless you specifically ask, and even then she offers the most succinct of answers. Her eldest daughter is twenty-two years old and a recipient of DACA. Her eleven-year-old daughter is an American citizen. Within the first few minutes of the first time we talked, a couple of weeks before my trip, she told me about having procured a cheap prescription for a yeast infection. On the phone, she was boisterous. In person, she is more subdued but warm. On her neck hangs a chain with a solid gold and ruby pendant of a salamander in honor of Luna, her pet salamander of seventeen years whom she saved from a pet store within days of arriving in the United States. Luna died a few months ago, and Julieta rests her hand on the pendant when she talks.

Julieta gives me instructions before we go in. We need to be careful because Macondo is one of a handful of pharmacies in Miami where uninsured immigrants can purchase prescription medication at inexpensive prices and without a prescription, and the people who run it wouldn't take kindly to questions from a stranger. These pharmacies run the clandestine operation from the back. "They know my face, I know their faces. They sell to me because of my accent. Whenever I need a medication that requires a prescription, I can get it there, though not very serious ones. They are very strict about some," Julieta explains. She tells me of a Dominican pharmacy elsewhere in Miami that sells a drug that helps addicts cope with withdrawal without a prescription. "They know they're doing something they shouldn't be doing, but they understand the human necessity," she says. "I have gone to them with my face swollen because of molar pain and they gave me something for the pain. I can go to Walgreens and they won't give me something even if I'm dying in front of them."

The pharmacy is run by a woman around sixty years old, who wears her hair down and blow-dried straight and puts on thick eye makeup behind her wire-rimmed glasses—impractical choices. "They call her a doctor but she doesn't do consultations," says Julieta. I am not allowed to ask her questions.

The pharmacy sells homeopathic ointments and creams. They also sell cleaning supplies, Central American folk dresses, pants sets in tiny sizes for children, and off-brand makeup. There are glass-enclosed shelves under lock and key, prudishly guarding condoms, yeast-infection treatments, and pregnancy tests. Julieta approaches a young woman who assists the doctor and who has "trained" at the pharmacy for many years. Julieta asks me for a symptom to relay to the young woman, and I describe a toothache, which I had in earnest the day before. I describe swollen gums where my wisdom teeth had been extracted, which the Internet tells me is a phantom pain. I ask Julieta if one might be able to purchase pain medication, and she asks for hospital-grade Tylenol. The young woman gives Julieta five pills in a small white envelope. We walk outside and stand on the street corner where we met, squinting in the sun and shielding our faces from the dust. She tells me that if I had walked into the pharmacy on my own, they would not have given me anything because of my accent. "Do you mean an Ecuadorian accent?" I ask leadingly. (My Spanish is telenovela Spanish: fluent, formal, regionally vague.) "Well, just your accent, they would have known not to trust you because of your accent," she says.

I ask Julieta if she ever resorts to alternative medicine in the absence of access to doctors, and she dismisses folk medicine as something that Cubans and Haitians do. "They have ridiculous beliefs with respect to medicine, and you're not going to leave them without them doing a prayer on you," she says. Instead, she describes another form of alternative medicine. "I have migraines and I have a Cuban neighbor who loves me. She was born here, and she's insured. She goes to her doctor and pretends she has migraines, she says that the light bothers her, that she throws up, and he gives her medication. She shares. A lot of people count on other people. My sister is a citizen and she gives her blood pressure medicine to a woman who is undocumented."

Julieta swears by hospital-grade Tylenol because she, too, sometimes gets intense pain in her molar. She goes to a Honduran man who was a dentist in his home country but cannot legally practice in the United States; instead he goes to private homes to fill cavities. "He does a very good job," she says. I have only a couple of dozen memories of my early childhood, and one is of my father writhing on the floor with tooth pain. My mother and I just stood back and watched, sometimes bending over to pat his arm, until the pain stopped—it took about a day. Either he would die from the pain or the pain would stop, and that time it stopped.

All my life, I have accompanied my parents to the doctor. I am their interpreter and advocate. They have gone to the emergency room only once, being pretty good about preventive healthcare and making regular appointments at the local community health center that sees low-income people on a sliding scale. For years, the chief doctor there was an Indian man who didn't speak great English and didn't speak great Spanish but who spoke with patients of all nationalities and languages without an interpreter anyway. He didn't like me and I didn't like him. When my mom was in her forties she found a lump in her breast, and he explained to me why ordering mammograms for women in their forties was a waste of resources, especially when the patient was uninsured and insurance couldn't pay for it, if you looked at the number of lives that early detection of breast cancer saved. *I don't think doctors are supposed to worry about the bottom line,* I tell him. *Didn't you take an oath?* I am maybe eighteen. *Aren't you smart,* he says. *That's her! She goes to Harvard,* my mom says. *That's right, motherfucker. I go to school in Boston. Well, not Boston. Cambridge. Just a little school in Cambridge. One day I'll make so much money that I'll pay for my mom's mammograms in cash, in crisp one-dollar bills, like a muhfucking kingpin. I'll buy this clinic and turn it into a museum for myself, in honor of me. I can hang up your children's diplomas for a special exhibition on children of doctors who go to state school, you cheap-ass motherfucker. I will ruin you.*

"She has history of breast cancer in her family" is what I actually said.

A lie.

"I'd appreciate it if you ordered one."

I have had the good fortune, mere dumb luck, to always have
had access to decent healthcare—New York City provides
low-cost insurance to minors in low-income families, and then
I went on to universities that provide insurance to their
students—and I view it with the awe and gratitude that only
someone who has seen healthcare rationed could appreciate.
When I was a child and I was sick, I went to the doctor. When
my parents got sick, I saw them breathe in the vapor from a
boiling pot of chamomile to moisten their inflamed bronchi, not
the most effective way of treating bronchitis. But you just said
your parents had access to the local community clinic, you say?
Sure, for preventive healthcare. Blood pressure, weight management, the common cold. My mother has low hemoglobin levels.
You can't get care for that on a sliding scale. In a *New York
Times* article from 2015 titled "Wary of Mainstream Medicine,
Immigrants Seek Remedies from Home," the author writes
wide-eyed about the use of medicinal herbs among immigrants
in New York who buy them at folk shops called botanicas.

But I don't find this reliance on folk medicine charmingly
idiosyncratic. Celebrating the treatment of illness with herbs
purchased at the same place where love potions are sold is curious to me, especially through the gaze of an outsider. Many
people I know, educated, well-off people, love alternative medicine. Whether the effect is real or placebo is not the pressing
issue here, so much as the matter of choice and access. Those
with resources might drink alternative tea treatments but will

ultimately have the choice to have their cancer treated with che-motherapy and not herbs, an option undocumented immigrants do not have.

But if you're going to try to treat an illness with herbs or prayer, you're probably going to have to frequent a botanica. Botanicas are named for the herbs sold inside shops that also stock oils, soaps, sprays, washes, statues, rosaries, amulets, books, and animal skulls. They're everywhere in immigrant neighbor-hoods. I wasn't allowed to go inside them as a kid because they were associated with dark magic. That's because for most of my childhood we were Catholic, and then Jehovah's Witness, while the belief systems that support the botanicas are vodou and Santería, two misunderstood religions that date back centuries. Santería and vodou were born when the Spaniards and French forced conquered peoples to convert to Catholicism but the peo-ple found a way to continue practicing their religions by com-bining them with Catholic iconography and rituals.

It is difficult to know how many botanicas there are in the United States because they are commonly registered as reli-gious or herbal stores (or pet shops, because they sell small ani-mals) and are thus not subject to the regulations that would apply to therapeutic establishments—including the need to register with the government, but that doesn't stop some Latinx people from using them for medical treatment.

In Miami, a woman named Esme—whom I met through Julieta—tells me she sometimes uses botanica herbs to treat ill-nesses, and I ask her to show me around some local botanicas. Esme is forty-nine years old and has lived in the United States for fourteen years. She has a dusting of freckles on her nose, with skin and hair the color of dull copper. Esme finds everything funny and her laughter is contagious. We meet at an overly air-conditioned Starbucks, where she orders a hot chocolate. "I'm a defender of alternative medicines," she says. But she erupts into laughter every time she mentions the herbs she used to treat a recent bout of pneumonia because she couldn't see a doctor. "I don't know what cured me, but I got better."

Her husband, Johnny, picks us up in his car. Unless you live in cities where immigrants can legally drive or in cities with excellent systems of public transportation, to be undocumented means you drive without a license in order to simply go about your day, which means always running the risk of being pulled over, charged, and deported. I am a little afraid when I get in the car because we could be stopped for literally anything, but I relax when I learn her husband is a permanent resident. We drive to the Great One Corporation, a large storefront with a garish seascape mural covering two walls. A mermaid that looks like Cher advertises that they are also florists. They do sell a lot of ceramics, but the only pets I can see are the small canaries in cages for sale along the entire length of a wall. "Oh, here's some linden blossom," Esme says as she points to a splintery yellow flower. "It's for nerves but it never works for me." There are baskets containing uva ursi, which looks a bit like holly, and yerba Buena. A tall porcelain figure of a black orisha named Obatala, the chief orisha and creator of human bodies, stands on a glass shelf. He is black, with a long, flowing gray beard, and wears a white turban and cloak. Underneath Obatala is a stash of brazilwood, said to cure diabetes, anemia, high blood pressure, and UTIs, and to be generally helpful in purifying blood. Nearby are piles of screwdrivers and hammers. Botanica Olocum is also a hardware store.

I approach two women behind the counter and ask them what they'd recommend for depression. They are both middle-aged. One of them has bleached hair. They look at each other and have an exchange under their breaths, then point to a stand containing books and pamphlets. I buy a small illustrated book printed on pulpy newsprint called *Cure Yourself of Alcoholism Through Natural Medicine*. It is part of a series inspired by the works of Dr. Edward Bach, the British doctor and homeopath whose eponymous flower remedies are foundational to homeopathic practice. (I remember a small glass vial of brand-name Bach white chestnut that I was gifted a couple of years ago by my in-laws. "Take two drops when thoughts and worries go round and round in your head," the bottle said. It was 27 percent alcohol, and after seeing a fat opossum cross the street one summer night when I was sitting on the porch I drank half the bottle. It was like taking a shot of tequila. I felt better.)

After Esme is done pointing out the useful herbs, we head back to the car. She and her husband hand me a gift: a small waxed-paper envelope containing a dream catcher and five energy stones. "These stones are not Santería," her husband explains to me. "This is what yogis do. The earth is vibrating and the stones have a different kind of vibration so they absorb different energies. The pharmaceutical company Bayer sent people to the Amazon to find indigenous cures for things and that's where they got their formulas. Of course, the problem with medicine now is that it doesn't cure illness. The doctor prescribes pills that won't cure you, just keep you a slave to other pills. They want patients to keep being patients. Medicine wants you to be a client." Her husband goes on and on and on as we drive to our next destination, and Esme doesn't say anything,

just laughs softly, which she does as easily as she breathes. A
little bit like Marilyn Monroe: a dark, girlish, worldly laugh.
We arrive at a small pharmacy next to a fried-chicken joint.
Another clandestine operation. Esme's husband approaches a
man behind the counter and says that I am a friend. I ask for
medications that I am either on or have at some point been on
so the feds can't accuse me of looking for drugs later. First, I ask
for Latuda, an antipsychotic. "Nope," he says. "That's an expensive one." Okay. Risperdal. "What dosage?" It's been a while, so
it's all muscle memory here. Three milligrams? He brings out a
bottle of brand-name Risperdal, which has $3 written on it in
marker. Maybe I can go back on Seroquel, I tell him.

"What dosage?"

Six hundred milligrams. He goes to the back for a few minutes and comes back with a white bottle of brand-name Seroquel with $5.50 written on it in marker. I thank him for showing
me my options and promise to come back later.

Seroquel and Risperdal are powerful antipsychotics. They're
tough drugs. Mean. The side effects can include akathisia (a
feeling of bodily restlessness), sedation, and increased levels of
the luteotropic hormone prolactin, a pregnancy hormone that
causes mammals to produce milk, even if they're not pregnant,
even if they're not female. In the long term, this can cause os-
teoporosis. There can be periods of nausea so bad you'll be prescribed antinausea meds used for patients on chemotherapy.
They can be lifesaving drugs, but require careful monitoring
and any changes should be incremental. I'm scared at the
thought of people taking these meds without supervision. Both
carry black-box warnings, the strictest possible FDA warning
that can appear on a drug's packaging. There's a potential in-

crease in suicidal thinking in youth, and elderly patients with dementia have exhibited higher rates of mortality, usually due to cardiac arrest or infection. The people who would resort to purchasing antipsychotics without a prescription at a pharmacy like this are not necessarily people who do not trust doctors due to cultural reasons. It's a different kind of people who would find themselves at a place like this—people who feel lucky to have found a shot at a miracle, even if the miracle risks deeper trouble than they can imagine.

Later that night, I take a cab to a lush, remote neighborhood outside Miami to attend a ceremony to initiate new priests and priestesses into vodou. I was invited by a local Haitian priestess named Roseline, a friend of a friend of someone I cold-called. I am generally unfriendly toward institutionalized religion, but vodou is a religion that was born out of anticolonial resistance— slaves in Haiti developed a spirit religion based on African, Native American, and Catholic beliefs, a true syncretism. Though French colonizers openly opposed it, slaves kept nurturing the belief system, creating a space where they could be free and where they could communicate with god through spirit inter-mediaries—so I have an open mind. At least, until I remember the caged canaries in the botanicas from earlier that day and become anxious about the possibility of witnessing an animal sacrifice. I suggest to Roseline that I am cowardly about "animal things." I say this delicately because I don't want to seem dis-missive of their ritual, but I am also having a hard time shaking my Western sensibilities. She obliges me by not responding. I regret asking about the animals.

During my first visit to Miami, there were rumors that the current administration will be rescinding TPS (temporary protected status) for Haitians, the program that allowed victims of the 2010 earthquake in Haiti to stay in the United States temporarily with a protected status, meaning they could live and work legally. The wait period before TPS expires is a crazy-making purgatory. I came to Miami just as many Haitians were contemplating what it might feel like to become undocumented and deportable overnight. People were scared. And scared people are vulnerable.

I arrive at the ceremony, which is held in a private home. I am so embarrassed about the animal question that I immediately try to compensate. I hug *everybody*. There are folding chairs fitted with white sheets and guests are wearing all-white everything. I'm wearing a black dress like a fool. I stand to the side and admire the artwork on the walls. There is a painting showing a group of topless women dancing near a large pig as a man approaches it with a sword. Someone dressed in all white hands me a Corona and asks me to put my notebook away. I approach a young man who seems about my age. He's leaning, and I like boys who lean. Jacob is tall and really cute and very warm and is actually so, so young. I learn that he is a priest already, that the spirit chose him when he was young, and in fact everybody at the ceremony either is, or is about to become, a houngan (priest) or mambo (priestess). "When people hear about vodou, they hear about negative stuff," he says, "but there are different branches. There is healing, there are treatments, there is protection. There is also bad stuff, but I focus on the good." He tells me about a friend who couldn't walk but after a vodou treatment is up and working. That sounds good to me, so I ask about cancer. "I was told there is a cure" is all he says. He knows a lot about herbs, so I ask where they're grown. "We grow them ourselves," he says. "Down here, in Florida, you can find plants on the side of the road. I also go to an old lady in Little Haiti to get herbs. She's a friend." He gives me specifics, which other people I speak to are reluctant to do—papaya leaf to keep your insides young, cerasee to clean out your system ("for example if you're on probation and can't be on drugs, this keeps the drugs out of the system"), sapo tea for diabetes, and vervain for low iron levels.

He walks me over to a dapper older man named Henri, who raves about vodou's medical efficacy. "They're the best antibiotics I know," Henri says. "There are herbs that can cure AIDS, high blood pressure, diabetes, swelling, blood clots, skin cancer—they just clean out your system," he says. He tells me I can find them at a botanica in Hialeah and he has friends who can grow them for free. "There is a leaf in the Amazon that cures cancer," he says. "Only Africans and Haitians know the cures." I ask how a cure for cancer could possibly be kept only among a small group of people. He doesn't know.

During the ceremony, a man dressed as a warrior holding a machete comes up to me and spits a liquid at me, which he says will bring success to everything I do. I overhear two people saying they don't trust me because I'm showing them too many pictures of my dog. There is a lot of alcohol at the ceremony—they bring out a strong blue drink, and I am told to drink it, and I do. I bond with some young mambos and houngans at the ceremony. I take down phone numbers. I'm fully aware of my surroundings, and I interview people about their experiences with vodou, but when my parents call me, they tell me my speech is slurred. I don't remember calling a taxi back to the hotel, but that's how I got home. In my room, I put on pajamas, take off my makeup, and go through my elaborate skin-care routine. It's weird. If I was drunk, I wouldn't even have brushed my teeth. When I wake up the next day, I am not hungover. But I do feel odd, kind of floating.

A year passes: I gain seventy pounds, eluding medical explanation. Miami is ravaged by Hurricanes Irma and Maria. ICE stops Greyhound buses and Amtrak trains to ask travelers for proof of citizenship. The #MeToo movement erupts. We buy special glasses for the first solar eclipse since 1918. (I stare directly into the sun because I'm drawn to self-harm.) White nationalists and neo-Nazis terrorize Charlottesville, Virginia, with motherfucking tiki torches and run a car into a young counterprotester named Heather Heyer, killing her. Trump says there were "some very fine people on both sides." My father starts disappearing on weekends, supposedly to go watch volleyball games at a local park, and my mom is too tired to deal, until he doesn't come home one weekend, and she and my brother call asking me to intervene.

My mother my mother my mother. My mother is a result of her mother's rape. Her mother abandoned her with *her* mother, who beat my mother with a vengeance and gave her permanent eye damage. When she was twelve she moved in with her very wealthy aunt and uncle and their three kids in the capital, away from the poor rural town where she was living with her grandmother. She adapted very well to the life of a rich adoptee. She was class president four years in a row and first in her class.

She hung out with the popular girls. She loved her friend Fernanda, who wore blue jeans ripped at the knee, which revealed just a sliver of the perfect tan year-round.

When my mother's biological father approached her at her high school graduation in Ecuador to say he was proud of her and ask that she take his last name, she told him to fuck off and kept her mother's maiden name. She idolized Hillary Clinton from the moment she laid eyes on her, which was shortly after a young Bill Clinton shook hands with my mother at a campaign stop in Brooklyn. When Hillary wore headbands, my mother wore headbands. When Hillary forgave her husband, my mother forgave my dad, too. When I was in the second grade, I got an 85 on a math test, and I hid the test from my parents. When my father found it, he took me on a car ride and explained that as a cabdriver he made a hundred dollars on good days and sometimes regardless of how hard he worked he would make fifteen dollars on a bad day, and it didn't make him any less of a person. My mother took me aside and asked me who the first man on the moon was. *Neil Armstrong*, I told her. Now name the second man on the moon. *I don't know*, I said. Nobody does, she said. If you're not number one, you're nothing.

My parents' apartment is railroad style, which means there are no doors. We have always had to shed our "outside clothes" because "outside clothes" are contaminated. My mother made us shower after being outside. When I was a child, and other children entered our home, she had them put on long socks and covered the couch with a cut-open trash bag before they could sit on it. She has taste outside her means. She'll starve for a week if it means she can buy herself a Chanel eye shadow. She likes to be photographed in front of tall buildings so she can emphasize her slim figure. She drinks her coffee with oat milk, no sugar. My father accuses her of secretly hating her coffee that dark but sticking to it because it makes her seem white. Never let a man tell you what you like or what you don't like, she told me on the phone the other day when I asked her for life advice.

I interviewed her for this book. She listed all of her life's regrets. I itemize them because she itemized them for me:

Marrying young.
Having a kid young.
Leaving me in Ecuador.
Not finishing college.
Not working out of the house when she was raising me.
Not having a career.

"I'm sorry," I say. "You've been such a good mom. I wouldn't be where I am without you. You made me."

"I understand I've been a good mother, but I want to know what it'd be like to be a successful woman on a personal level, not on the level of a mother," she responds.

Since we met, Esme has become a surrogate for motherly warmth. We text regularly. I am genuinely happy to see her again when I visit Miami a year later. I ask Esme to meet me at her favorite restaurant, an Italian place in a fashionable shopping district in downtown Miami. Everyone there is Cuban. Esme orders squash ravioli and a glass of orange juice. We talk about the new activist group she cofounded and presides over as vice president, a local group of mostly housekeepers called Mujeres en Solidaridad. They hold know-your-rights workshops and teach domestic workers about gender-based violence.

She talks to me about the disappeared. All Latin Americans know about the disappeared. The period of the late 1970s and 1980s was a dark time in South America. It was a time of military dictatorships in Argentina, Uruguay, and Chile. The governments kidnapped civilians and took them to undisclosed locations and tortured and killed them. Their bodies were never found. Their bones were never found. In Argentina, in just seven years' time, the government disappeared about thirty thousand people. They woke up one morning and went about their days and then they vanished without a trace. So in Argentina, their mothers formed a group called the Mothers of the Plaza de Mayo. They wore white scarves around their heads and marched two by two in front of the presidential palace every Thursday afternoon at 3:30 P.M. holding pictures of their disappeared children. They still do it every Thursday afternoon. These mothers are legendary. They have been marching for forty years.

Esme is undocumented and Uruguayan. She grew up during the dictatorship of Gregorio Álvarez. Some women in Mujeres en Solidaridad are Argentine, and they feel that in their adopted country of America, undocumented immigrants are being disappeared into the silence when they go into their routine check-ins at the U.S. Citizenship and Immigration Services offices in nearby Miramar. The immigrants are treated like livestock, they don't allow them to use the bathroom or sit on the floor during days-long waits, and they often just ship them to detention centers, never to be seen again. So Esme and some other ladies formed a subgroup called You Are Not Alone, and they stand across the street from the Miramar USCIS offices and invite immigrants in line to approach them for coffee, water, doughnuts, ponchos, and phone chargers. Esme saw a woman give birth waiting in line in hundred-degree weather. *We see you, and you won't get away with this!* the women yell at officers.

Esme's father was a revolutionary under the Álvarez dictatorship. At eight o'clock in the evening, when the country went dark for curfew, people came over to her house to plot by candlelight against the dictatorship. She still feels panic when she hears helicopters overhead, remembering being shoved under tables or pushed into shallow canals when they heard choppers. "Of course, the only thing that matched my father's revolutionary spirit was his violent temper, which was worse when he drank," she says. "His beatings were barbaric. I've been a survivor ever since I was a baby. I was born premature and I was born a girl. He wanted a boy."

His beatings would leave her nearly bedridden. The last time he laid a finger on her was when she was nineteen years old. She grabbed a knife and confronted him with it. "That's when I realized I was capable of anything," she says. She had boyfriends who abused her psychologically and sexually, but she didn't recognize it as domestic violence until she began volunteering at shelters for women. "When I began leading workshops about abusive relationships, I was like *oh my god.*" She's never told her husband about her experiences with sexual assault because she's afraid of what he'll say. "You know men," she tells me. "He'll ask me what I was wearing or something. I don't trust him not to say that. So there's no catharsis in the home."

I tell her my parents are having a moment.

"You know what?" she says. "I don't have the spirit of a home-maker. I wasn't born for the kitchen. I hate household chores. When I was little, I used to tell my mother, *I wasn't born for this, I was born to be a musician*. And she'd tell me, *Even violinists have to cut potatoes*, and she'd send me to the kitchen. I loved to study. I loved to travel. I'm ambitious. I'm fascinated by the world. But I had an accident at the factory where I worked and after that I stayed at home while my husband worked, and when that's your dynamic, you have to earn your keep. Food has to be on the table. Laundry has to be done. Your mouth has to be shut. I always rebel, but then there's the guilt. Rebelling has its price."

We order dessert. She orders a tiramisu and shows me pictures of her recent trip to New York in support of a boycott and protest by female agricultural workers in Florida. Esme participated in a hunger strike—okay, it was more of a fast—and she's still on a high from the adrenaline. She couldn't fly there, because she doesn't have a state ID, so she took a chartered bus, with other undocumented women like her. She was scared every minute of the twenty hours she was on the bus that ICE was going to stop them. When she finally got out of the bus and was able to breathe in the freezing New York air, she felt alive again. She seems almost hysterical as she tells me this.

She leans into me. "The truth is that to me the immigration advocacy is almost secondary," she confides. "We've helped shy women who clean other people's homes and pick up after their husbands to leave their homes and deliver press conferences, do TV interviews, have meetings with congresspeople. We had a gala, and I said, 'Ladies, you don't have to go smelling like Clorox. Be glamorous!' And they did. You should have *seen us*, with our hair done and our gowns, rubbing elbows with lawyers and doctors and politicians. We get women out of the home and give them a reason to exist."

I wonder what it would take for my mom to feel alive again, to have a reason to exist. She only gets dressed up to go to the Kingdom Hall and I usually tease her like, "Mom, Jesus thinks you look great, that's enough highlighter," but I know she's actually dressing up for church because she has nowhere else to go other than work and it makes me feel guilty.

That night, I travel to Miramar to see a mambo named Naomie whom Jacob recommended. She is his spiritual sister, and she says she can give me a cleansing treatment to protect me against ICE—for a price. This sounds to me like a notario, someone who claims they can fix people's immigration papers for a steep price but is not licensed to practice law. They are vultures in the immigrant community.

Miramar is about a half hour away from the hotel where I am staying. The hotel is inside Dolphin Mall, one of Miami-Dade's largest malls, which is packed with outlet stores and Cuban men manning As Seen on TV kiosks who try to guess your country of origin ("Mami, you look Peruvian, are you Peruvian?") and offer to straighten your hair with a mini ceramic flat iron. I take a stroll through the mall every day, and every day I see people taking paraplegic family members out for a window-shopping excursion and paletas, and against the backdrop of loud club beats it makes me sad. I'm just this sad bitch.

In the cab, I get a text from Jacob telling me to bring a bottle of Tito's and a pack of Newport cigarettes. He says he's coming too. *Oh, cool, what are you getting done?* I ask. "Who's going to translate for you and how are you going to understand what the spirit is going to say to you?" he says. Naomie's apartment complex is checkered with lush grass; ducks happily peek their heads out of bushes and newts and geckos scurry up and down walls. She doesn't live far from the USCIS check-in facility that Esme told me about, the site of the abuses against immigrants. The cleanse costs $277.77.

I meet Jacob outside Naomie's apartment. He makes me feel safe. He has a strong, grounding presence and he smells like cigarettes. Naomie interviews me before the rite. She asks me what afflicts me. *Oh man.* I tell her that I write about immigration and worry I can't protect the people I write about. I would like to protect them, or at least not have nightmares about ICE. That's true and feels like a safe thing to share, although I don't go into detail. As a rule, I try to not tell strangers my nightmares unless I'm being paid by the word.

I'm not sure what to think. I'm curious about vodou because of its anticolonial roots but I also believe an immigration cleanse is bullshit because nobody can protect anybody from ICE, and this cleanse is expensive and the Haitians who would ask for an immigration cleanse in Miami right now are probably scared shitless about losing TPS. Is Naomie a notario? Maybe. But maybe one with powers.

Naomie writes down some notes on a square of white paper. This will be my plea to the spirit she will invoke. She is barefoot and her toenails are painted bright yellow. The apartment is very hot, and my mascara melts and gathers on my bottom eyelashes. There are two chairs facing each other. Naomie sits in one; I sit in the other. A large piece of red silk is laid out on the floor, along with white candles, a set of tcha-tcha rattles (kind of like maracas wrapped in colorful beads), the notepaper with my plea to the spirit, and various huge bottles of alcohol. A gallon jug of Tito's Vodka stuffed with hot peppers. A bottle of perfume. The requested pack of Newports. Naomie powders her face with a chalk-white powder. Jacob is seated beside Naomie and begins chanting in Creole and French, and Naomie closes her eyes. The air gets still and then she collapses and begins to shake. Her eyes roll to the back of her head. Then she sits upright again, and she opens her eyes and it's like she's this new person. That's because, Jacob says, she has been inhabited by a male spirit. She slouches on her chair, leaning back with swagger and her legs apart, and lights a cigarette. (That's another thing about vodou. Men are often inhabited by female spirits and women by male spirits. Vodou spirits are said to protect and nurture queer people, unlike Christian denominations that persecute members of the LGBTQ community in Haiti.) Her eyes are black black black, and her powdered white face has taken on the form of a mask. She speaks to me through Jacob, who translates between English and Creole.

The spirit's name is Emmanuel. He is one of Naomie's ancestors. He takes a swig of his favorite drink and offers some to Jacob. Jacob takes a swig, then coughs a lot. I drink a tiny little bit. It tastes like gasoline smells. Naomie makes me wash my hands in perfume, then moves the chair aside, and I kneel on the red silk sheet as she blows smoke all over me—when the smoke is blown in my face, I exhale instead of inhaling, I'm not getting dizzy—and rubs perfume on my neck and back. They light the piece of paper with my plea on fire and combine the ashes with the spirit's favorite drink. They ask me to take one swig from the bottle in every cardinal direction, and I tell Jacob to tell Emmanuel that I didn't have lunch and too much alcohol would make me throw up. They put the drink in a water bottle and say to drink it when I get home after I put some food in my stomach. The spirit asks me if I am worried about anybody in particular. I tell him yes, many people in particular. After a few back-and-forths, Jacob says Emmanuel has offered to turn me into a protective shield, and that he will offer me guidance via dreams, déjà vu, the way the wind blows, the flutter of my heart, and hunches.

The vodou spirit wants to know if I'm satisfied. He wants to know how I'm willing to *show* that I'm satisfied, how much his offered protection against ICE means to me. I take this to mean the mambo wants me to put a price on how much this cleansing meant to me by paying more than the $277.77. I tell them I only brought $280 in cash, but that I was a writer and thus, my words being currency—*the worst pickup line in the world*—I offer to recite for the spirit, Emmanuel, a poem. I know some Emily Dickinson poems by heart, I tell him. They're love poems but they're not about a boy, they're about Death, I tell him. Jacob takes a long time to explain this to the spirit, and Emmanuel, chalk-white and boozy, makes a face, aghast, then another face—disgusted. He does *not* want me to recite a poem. I know they were just asking me for more money. Notario shit. A few months later, Jacob texts me out of the blue. He needs me to loan him some money. He doesn't explain why, and when I tell him I don't even lend money to family, he stops responding.

Salome Allende is a friend of Esme's, a fellow member of the domestic worker advocacy group Mujeres en Solidaridad. She is forty-eight years old and Argentine. Her husband died of brain cancer in 2012 after being turned away by every local hospital they approached because he was uninsured. Overnight, she became the family's sole breadwinner.

When we speak on the phone a few weeks before my first visit, Salome cries, puts her hand on the mouthpiece to try to block the sound of it, and tells me she wants to show me the notebook her dead husband kept during his last weeks alive to keep track of his treatments. After we hang up, I text her U.S. Census data showing that children of immigrants have higher rates of college and postgraduate education graduation than other groups, and she says my texts make her feel good. She has four children, one of whom has DACA. I am a one-trick pony, unable to comfort with anything other than grades.

Salome is tall, with straight dark-brown hair and the intense feminine air I associate with perfumed talcum powder. She has been in the United States for seventeen years, working mostly as a housekeeper for hotels and apartments. She has four pugs: fourteen-year-old Tobin and her three puppies, Megan, Alex, and Ashlyn, named for members of the U.S. Women's National Soccer Team. "I like to lie down on the couch and let them climb all over me," she says. She sleeps curled on her side with Tobin at her chest, Megan on the backs of her knees, and Alex on her back. Ashlyn has been staying with her daughter.

Salome was fifteen and sheltered when she met Harrison, a lone Argentine. He was a year older. His parents were not around, which led him to a fierce and early independence. Salome describes her own parents as authoritarians who had two expectations of her: go to school and return home to take care of her younger siblings, which meant no boyfriends or even friends. But Harrison drew her in. "Meeting him was like a soap opera," she says. After the two dated secretly for a year, Harrison tried to talk to her parents but they wouldn't listen. So she ran away with him and they got married. "In retrospect, they just wanted me to study, like any parents would. I thought it was love at the time, but it was an escape," she says. "My own kids don't know that story," she adds, sounding surprised by her own words. "They always ask me how we met and I tell them their dad was taking a stroll when he passed me standing in a doorway. I just don't want them to do the same thing."

They had four kids who became their whole lives. On weekends, they'd go to the beach or to the park to play soccer. They threw parties at home and danced with one another. "Everything that we didn't have ourselves growing up, we gave to our children," she says. In Miami, Harrison worked in construction near a chemical plant. After two years at the job, he got sick. "At first, we thought it was a cough, and we didn't want to waste money, so we didn't go to the doctor. He'd just take aspirin." When he finally went, doctors said he would need chemotherapy immediately. The hospital asked about legal status. When the family said he didn't have papers, the hospital turned him away. So did cancer treatment centers. "I said, 'Am I supposed to take my husband home and wait for him to die?'" she says. Did they seem sorry? "They were cold. Totally cold."

Salome's friend recommended a woman from Miami Beach who described herself as a naturalist. They had nothing to lose. Joanne was tall and blond and said she had cured stage-four cancer patients with her treatments. She began making changes to Harrison's diet, instructing them to eat organic and buy exotic fruits they had to drive all over Miami to find. "When you want to hold on to someone, when it's time for them to go but

you don't want to believe it, you go and find the exotic fruits,"
explains Salome. One morning, we drive to a Latin American
diner in Little Havana and order Colombian breakfast platters
of fried eggs, black beans, cream, and arepas. The coffee is light
and sweet. Bodega coffee. Un café regular is the same anywhere.
Salome takes a marble-speckled notebook out of her purse and
pushes it to me. It is a record of the naturalist's treatment, some
in Harrison's large shaky handwriting, in Spanish, and some in
their daughter Olivia's handwriting, girlish and in English. She
was sixteen at the time.

*All the tea you can drink. Miracle oatmeal. Stopped vomiting and
soothed stomachache.* Girlish, bubbly handwriting.

Chew the juices as if they were solid food for 15 minutes before bed.
I imagine Harrison pretending to chew liquid for fifteen minutes, his jaw muscles tightening, the fluids dribbling through
his lips, feeling like an idiot, showing his family he was putting
up a fight, maybe believing it himself.

I am doing everything I can to stay alive.

Harrison's brain tumors affected his memory so he often forgot he had cancer. Salome had to break the news to him over
and over, until she stopped. When the pain overwhelmed him,
they took him to the hospital, because the ER can't reject anyone. The doctors gave him morphine and then sent him home.
By this point they were paying out of pocket. Shortly before he
died, his heart filled up with water and the hospital recommended open-heart surgery. Post-operation, his children took
turns taking care of him because Salome was now working long
days as a housekeeper.

"Why operate on his heart if he had at most six months to
live?" she asks. "Medicine is a total mafia."

Harrison died in 2012. The cancer had spread to his throat and lungs. His blood was infected. He was forty-six years old.

Salome knows the naturalist's treatment didn't cure him, but she thinks it gave him a better quality of life during his final three months. "We put faith in the natural," Salome says. "We had to. Some people choose between the medical and the natural, but we didn't have the funds for the medical. We could not even go to the hospital for his convulsions. So we chose the natural." She lives alone now and does her best to keep busy. "When my husband died, I was low. I was in this country alone with four kids and little work. I thought about going back to Argentina. But I said, you know what, I'm not the first this has happened to and I'm not the last." Every conversation with Salome ends the same way—with the metaphor of the sacrificial lamb. "Quite literally, my husband gave his life for his children so they could have a future," she says. "My son promised him over his grave that he was going to study and get his degree, and now he's working a part-time job and studying."

By the time I go to Miami the second time, she has obtained a green card through her citizen son. I notice her confidence immediately. I ask her if she feels differently. "Since getting my green card, I'm honestly more defiant. If a cop were to stop me, I'd ask, *Why are you stopping me?* If there is a car accident, I have insurance now, so I say, *Call the cops if you want.* Once, I got into a car accident back when I was undocumented, and my son had to rush over with four hundred dollars in cash so the other driver wouldn't involve the police. I just have more confidence and better self-esteem now."

One night, we drive to a small Cuban bar in Little Havana

that bills itself as home of the world's most famous mojito. They
serve it smoking and with a cane sugar straw. A band of Carib-
bean men in fedoras sing salsa by Rubén Blades and Héctor
Lavoe. Salome orders a lime-green margarita with a tiny pink
umbrella. I ask her how she's doing, aside from the newfound
security of her green card. "Well, I'm doing things I should
have done at age twenty or twenty-five. I moved out of my dad's
house at age sixteen and then moved into my husband's. But I
have my own place now. What I didn't live then, I live now," she
says. She tells me about her children, and cries a little because
they miss their father. "Anyway, let's go party," she says. I think
she's joking, that she's taking me back to my hotel, but she's
actually taking me to drive around Wynwood, a former warehouse district that's become Miami's hottest nightlife spot. We
drive around the whole neighborhood multiple times, in circles,
and she gasps and murmurs under her breath about how much
she loves graffiti art, which covers the façades of all the night-
clubs. She's in ecstasy. At some point, I start stifling yawns because it's almost midnight, and she scolds me for having
surrendered to the life of an old woman when I am so young.
She points out girls in high heels and tiny dresses in long lines
by the bouncers. "Oh my god, they look *amazing*," she says. She
says she wants us to come back the following night, this time
with Esme and a woman named Isadora, the current president
of Mujeres en Solidaridad.

Salome picks me up early the next evening. First stop, her
dance studio. She wants me to meet Uriel, the instructor. He's
Cuban and there is an enormous portrait of him, bulging out of
a tuxedo, showing off a gaudy gold watch and a hand tattoo, on

the door of the studio. At the top of the stairs is a cluster of middle-aged women in leggings, flip-flops, and tank tops with the same logo, the image of pinups in bikinis, and they all greet Salome with a kiss on each cheek. "Half of us are older women," Salome says. "We're all women who have never done this before. I certainly didn't do this when my husband was alive. Uriel tells us to leave our demons at the door, and that's right where you'll find mine. Dance class has become my church, my therapy." I don't meet Uriel, who is busy teaching simple salsa moves to a line of women, but I do meet his wife, who walks slowly on account of her recent liposuction. (On Mondays, everyone in the class wears tank tops with the logo of her cosmetic surgeon's practice.) Uriel crossed the U.S.–Mexico border a couple of years ago and he was granted political asylum because he's Cuban.

Do you know about the "wet foot, dry foot policy"? Miami's politics and demographics were forever changed by it. In 1995, Bill Clinton introduced a revision of the Cuban Adjustment Act of 1966, the pillar of this new version being the wet foot, dry foot policy, which ordered that the American Coast Guard not intercept Cubans in the water midway between Cuba and the United States, but should anyone successfully arrive on solid land, they could remain in the United States and have expedited routes to permanent resident status and citizenship. This policy applied to entries on soil too. Sometimes Cuban émigrés took flights to Central America, then made their way to the U.S.–Mexican border. If they were detained in the crossing, they could show their Cuban passports and would then be separated from the Mexicans and Central Americans to be processed for asylum, which didn't add to the general goodwill among other

Latin American immigrants. Barack Obama ended the policy on January 12, 2017. "We were lucky," Uriel's wife tells me.

"But we're immigrants too. We're all immigrants," she adds.

We're on our way to pick up Esme in Hialeah when Salome tells me she and her husband were married twice. They were divorced for two years. "Marriages that come here split up unless the women don't work," she tells me. "And I worked, so it caused some problems. We split up, we divorced, we had separate apartments; I was really getting used to my life as a single woman. Then he calmed down, and said he missed me, and would serenade me with his guitar. We started living together again, and I was okay with that arrangement, but he wanted to get married again so we could be together forever."

We pick up Esme, who can't contain her excitement when she gets in the car. We're now on our way to pick up Isadora. It's 9:00 P.M. Esme gets a call from her husband and son. "I'm with the girls. I left food on the stove for you," she whispers.

Isadora lives an hour away. Now it's ten o'clock. Isadora gets in and excitedly tells us she wants to drive by some mansions that "belong to these sheikhs." She is wearing a fuchsia top, silver hoop earrings so big they touch her shoulders, and hair teased up like Dolly's. They marvel at the mansions, and Isadora says she takes long strolls in expensive neighborhoods whenever she feels depressed. "Oh god, not me," says Esme. "I look at mansions and get stressed just seeing them because I think I'll have to clean them." Salome doesn't like using the GPS and only Isadora knows this area, so I have no idea where they're taking me. At some point, amid the chisme, it becomes clear we're taking a long trip out of town to a casino. I tell them I have a five o'clock flight the following morning, and so they downgrade their ambitions for the night; Isadora gives us turn-by-turn directions to a nearby Fort Lauderdale tiki bar across from the beach.

Isadora is interested in the punch bowl. I say it's literally a fishbowl of rum and she gets a devilish look in her eye. While browsing the menu, as small talk, she tells me she was an international affairs lawyer in Bolivia, specializing in Russian relations. She lived in Russia for six years and is fluent in Russian. Now she has been here sixteen years and is a housekeeper. "It's fine!" she says. "I knew what I was getting into." Isadora and Salome want to try gator. "COCODRILO?" they ask. They cover their mouths and stifle screams. We decide to get mojitos that come in commemorative glasses. "That's nice of them, but I was going to take the glass home anyway," Esme says.

Let's talk shop. People think cleaning houses is easy, but it's a dangerous job. None of them have been personally assaulted, but they all know women who have been groped or raped on the job, who have had their wages stolen, who have been psychologically abused and then forced into silence by employers who threatened to call ICE on them. One housekeeper put the wrong PIN in the security system to get into a house, the cops came, they alerted immigration, and she was deported. Housekeepers are exposed to so many temperature fluctuations between rooms, between jobs, between industrial freezers and industrial ovens, that some of them have facial paralysis. To clean an oven, you need to turn it on, and the chemicals smoke up. You try not to breathe in those fumes, but they sometimes get inside the paper masks anyway. Housekeepers suffer from migraines, from rashes. Salome tells the story of working for an elderly couple for fifteen years. After the wife dies, the husband remarries a woman with the early stages of dementia. She loses a ring her mother gave her, not even gold, *costume jewelry*, and she accuses Salome of having taken it. Salome comes to the house to help her look for it, and finds it undisturbed on the piano. "You planted it there!" the woman screams. "You stole it, and you put it back!" Her husband looks down on the floor, not doubting Salome but not wanting to upset his wife. Salome quits on the spot. "I've never been so humiliated in my life," she says. "Like I'd throw away my livelihood for a piece of costume jewelry."

I ask the women how often they have nightmares. This has become one of my favorite questions to ask.

How many years have you spent in this country?
How often do you have nightmares?

Every night, they say. Esme dreams about concentration camps nightly, about having to hide people in her home, people who can't make a sound. There was a time when she was so anxious that she could not fall asleep, so she would have a glass of wine, then another, then another, and before she knew it a whole bottle would be gone. "My dad was an alcoholic, so I shut that down," she says. I tell them about my nightmares, about my mental issues, and say how grateful I am for my medication. "Couldn't you just decide to *not* be a victim to those things?" Esme asks me. "Couldn't you promise yourself you won't succumb to your demons? I did that," she says. "I've trained myself not to give in. The only thing that I can't get rid of is that I take four showers a day, and I won't touch food that belongs to certain categories I've created, but that's all."

"That . . . sounds like OCD," I say.

"If they give us papers, psychiatrists will get rich because we're all crazy," Isadora says. We all laugh.

"Sweet Home Alabama" comes on the bar radio.

"I *love* this song," Esme says. "I call it 'Sweet Home Hialeah.'" She starts to sing at the top of her lungs. She may be tipsy. Some of the other patrons at the bar, white people, look at us, and it makes me nervous, and it makes me sad that it makes me nervous. I imagine one of them taking out an AK-47 and shooting us down, then walking over to our bodies, then shooting us in our heads, execution style, as we continue to sing the pretty redneck song, marveling at the mansions surrounding us, trying not to think of cleaning them, and then, as I feel those white stares on us, I pour a drink on my head. The girls cheer and I let out a bloodcurdling scream. My first ever.

CHAPTER 4

Flint

I first visited Flint in 2017, a year after it made national head-lines for having lead in its water and two months after a court charged five high-profile officials, including the director of the Michigan Department of Health and Human Services, Nick Lyon, and the chief medical executive for the department, Eden V. Wells, with involuntary manslaughter for their role in misleading the public about water safety. I wanted to see what it looks like when the state poisons its own people.

Long before the water crisis, Flint had found itself in dire straits. Throughout the 1990s, General Motors, which once employed half of Flint, closed almost all of its factories in the city. By 2014, half of the population had left—autoworkers, their families, and the people who survived on feeding, clothing, and entertaining the autoworkers and their families. The people in Flint now are the people who did not leave, because they could not or did not want to. Fewer than one hundred thousand people live in the city today, down from its height of two hundred thousand in the 1960s. In 2016, 45 percent of Flint residents lived below the poverty line, the highest rate in the country for cities with more than sixty-five thousand residents.

As the city got smaller and blacker and browner and poorer, public services crumbled. Firefighters and police have been cut, and arson is rampant. Garbage collection has been privatized. One out of nine houses in Flint is vacant. City residents have to pay astronomic water-bill prices to pay for services the city is providing, even though the water is still bad. For many families, backed-up bills run into the hundreds of dollars. Some churches try to help by writing checks.

The undocumented community in Flint has been affected by the water crisis in disturbingly specific ways. Flyers announcing toxic levels of lead in the Flint waterways were published entirely in English, and when canvassers went door-to-door to tell residents to stop drinking tap water, undocumented people did not open their doors out of fear that the people knocking were immigration authorities. (There had reportedly been a raid at a grocery store the week before the news broke.) When President Obama declared a state of emergency, the National Guard was deployed to Flint, making undocumented people even less likely to open the door, since this time the canvassers were in uniform. Some undocumented Flint residents learned of the lead in their water only when family members from Mexico called them on the phone to ask about it. They had seen reports of the poisoned water on Univision.

Laura Mugavero, leader of a local community organization that serves immigrants, picks me up from my hotel and we drive downtown to a homey hole-in-the-wall Mexican restaurant.

Laura has '80s-era curly hair dyed a coppery brown. Lady mags generally say that women must pick eyes or lips to emphasize but she has picked both—very dark eye shadow, very red lipstick. We order drinks. She sends back the salsa because it is too mild. The owner of the restaurant, whose husband knows Laura from her work in the community, comes over personally to say the restaurant is popular among white people and they are the reason the salsa is too mild. She then apologizes and brings over two hotter, spicier options.

Laura was born in Mexico to a migrant worker father and a mother who eventually achieved legal status through the 1986 amnesty. She was nine years old when she crossed the border with her parents and her baby sister. She holds back tears as she remembers watching her mother fall into the Rio Grande before finding sturdier ground and making it across. They eventually made their way to Flint, where her father was hired by a GM auto plant on the spot. It was 1994, just a few years before GM closed its final car plants.

The city is different now. After dinner, we drive around East Flint, the Latinx part of town, and she points out where her childhood home would be if it hadn't been demolished, and where her schools had been, all of them now shut down. There used to be four high schools in the area, but two closed down. Even with the population flight, the remaining two schools are overcrowded. Here was the carcass of a grandfather clock factory. Here was where Buick City once stood, 235 acres of factory grounds now surrounded by a chain-link fence and barbed wire, and overrun by pink weeds. Here was the old General Motors Institute of Technology, where they sent engineers, its name hardly visible on the stone. They had tried to turn the

Chevy plant into a park, but instead it just sits there, weeds and vodka bottles. Empty plastic water bottles have become so abundant that people shove them into the spaces in their wire fencing, so yards and lots look like modern art exhibits. Houses, apartments, and trailers are boarded up with graffiti and children's rocking horses sit dirty and spooky on the lawn.

I make plans to attend Sunday mass with Margarita Davila at a church that proudly bills itself as the only one in the area that offers Spanish services. Margarita is a sixty-eight-year-old Mexican American immigration activist with small rimless glasses and short, curly blond hair. She picks me up from my hotel in her red pickup truck, a jewel-encrusted rosary hanging from the mirror. St. Aloysius is located right outside Flint proper and the faithful have to make the drive. Today they will be celebrating First Communion for the kids.

On our way we pick up Cesar, a Venezuelan man in the middle of a political asylum petition who has no car. The week before, he had attempted to take the city bus, but public transportation is not reliable here, and he showed up at 11:00 A.M. for an eight o'clock mass. He tells me he was an optometrist back home. Once he is alone with me, he touches my arm and whispers, "We are not all Mexican immigrants." He writes down his name and number and slips it to me.

Today's worshippers form a line at the entrance of St. Aloysius Church, and each of us dips two fingers into the holy water as we walk in, then we make the sign of the cross on our foreheads, lips, and chests. Parents are taking pictures of their kids dressed like little brides and groomsmen, all in white for First Communion.

When you walk through Flint the most striking aspect of the streetscape, second only to boarded-up houses, is the sheer number of bars and churches. I ask Margarita if Flint residents are especially religious, and she says they just need the services the churches provide because the state is so absent. Despite the horror of it all, she says the water crisis has made more services available to them. "They finally realized we were here," she says.

A few undocumented church members gather to meet me in the church auditorium after services, and we sit down at a table for doughnuts and black coffee in Styrofoam cups. They sit with their hands folded in front of them, their posture boot-camp perfect. Margarita had made a post on the church's Facebook page announcing my visit, and it's not exactly how I'd have described myself (self-made cult escapee) but how other people like to describe me (Yale PhD student) and that shit is distancing. They know what I'm here to ask them and they are ready to talk.

They spread their arms wide to show me how the auditorium was filled with donated cases of water when the story first hit the news. "As far as the eye can see," a woman tells me. "I always said the reason we were getting help was that we were in the news, but they'd see as time passed. I knew it was all going to disappear." The auditorium is now empty.

"I'm grateful to have water at all because many people in this world don't have water," says a woman named Lilliana. Before we talk about the poisoned water, they begin by discussing blessings. Lilliana begins with her blessings—I later learn Lilliana is fighting cancer—and only after I've revealed my own blessings am I allowed to carry on with questions. "Well, first there were the rumors," she says. "We suspected something was very wrong." The water was the color of rust and tasted like actual shit but when residents called city officials, they were told they were crazy. Then General Motors stopped using Flint-sourced water at one of their remaining truck plants because they feared the water would corrode the parts. Junior, Lilliana's son, says GM employees told their own families about the water but word did not get out. Junior has papers. One of his jobs is to go door-to-door installing filtration systems and teaching people how to use them. He knows that some people in the Latinx community are undocumented, so he tends to ask his co-workers to stay in the car while he goes alone and deals with the paperwork. He motions on an imaginary iPad the scrolling and skipping he has to do for people without Social Security numbers. They tell him they don't trust him because he's with the water company—with the city. "But I tell them, what? Soy raza. I'm just like you. I've got you."

"There is a huge problem with trust in the community," says Margarita. "The state can say the water is made out of gold, and people still wouldn't drink it."

Lilliana's daughter, Karen, says that all of her children's blood tests for lead came back with the same level. Then her test came back with the exact same level, as did her mother's, her father's, then everybody else's. Everyone's was identical. Karen asked around in the community, and her neighbors reported the same level as well. The tests were run by the Environmental Protection Agency and the Michigan Department of

Environmental Quality. "When I saw that the tests were being run from the state, I said, how could I possibly trust you?"

"Even if the level was true, it's inaccurate because what they don't tell you is that when lead enters your body, it doesn't just stay in your blood, it goes into your bones, it digs really deep, and tests don't detect that," says Lilliana. Research has found that exposure to lead in childhood can have devastating long-term effects like high blood pressure, kidney damage, and intellectual disabilities including challenges with speech, language comprehension, memory, fine-motor skills, and behavioral self-control. Because children of color are much more likely to be exposed to lead at a young age, it is devastating to think about what will happen to an entire generation of Flint children. What promises can you make to a child about the world of possibility ahead of them when the state has poisoned their bloodstreams and bones such that their behavioral self-control and language comprehension are impaired? How many graves has the government of Michigan set aside for the casualties of the water crisis that will end with a gunshot in fifteen years' time? We all know how cops respond to kids of color with intellectual disabilities or mental illness.

Having to use bottled water makes everything about running a household more difficult. Lilliana goes through four or five cases of water a day. The youngest grandchildren cry and tell her she is mean because she gives them quick lukewarm showers and has prohibited baths. "If you use hot water, the hot water opens your pores and the lead gets absorbed through your skin," she says. "Many people say that your skin doesn't absorb lead, that you only absorb it through your stomach, but that's just not true. Hot water opens your pores and it gets way down deep in there. So lukewarm and cold-water showers it is."

Lilliana left Mexico for the United States twenty years ago and is my mother's age. She used to work in housekeeping until she got sick, and now she stays at home taking care of her five grandchildren. She does not know whether her breast cancer, newly diagnosed as of two months ago, after years of clean self-exams and annual mammograms, has any correlation to the leaden water, but she is an optimist and a master of avoidance, so she does not want to talk about the possibility.

"After moving to Michigan, like many immigrants, I kept saying, *Next year I'll leave, next year I'll leave, next year I'll leave,* and I never left. It's all a lie. I don't love Flint, but I do love Michigan. I love the greenery. I love nature. And there are so many birds in Michigan. My husband gets upset with me because I get up out of bed at dawn every morning to go watch the birds wake up. I like rising with the birds. I like to hear them sing." I ask Lilliana if she owns pet birds. There is a long pause. "I don't *own* birds. I set them free.

"You see, my husband got me some small birds as a present but I don't like them in cages so I went outside one day and I released them. I had two blue birds and one green bird. I wanted my birds to be wild so I never even named them. They kept returning to my yard. I used to talk to them about how their day was going. I asked them when they were hungry. They were very attentive."

It was her son who told her she had cancer. There's nothing strange about children of immigrants serving as interpreters for their parents at doctors' appointments, but on this day the doctor spoke to her son for a long time and she knew from the look on their faces that something was wrong. Then the doctor hugged her and said, Lo siento. The Spanish word for "cancer" is "cancer," but he left it to her son to tell her the news. She went home to be alone, she wanted to be alone, but who could be alone in a house teeming with family. "I didn't want to tell anyone. I said to myself, *I'll treat it and it'll be fine. I'll get out of this.* I have always moved forward and removed every obstacle in my path." She learned everything about the disease and asked all the right questions. But then the doctors told her to go back to Mexico because the radiation would be too expensive here and she wouldn't be able to pay out of pocket. Junior asked her if she wanted to go back. She said, "I'm not going anywhere."

Lilliana starts chemotherapy shortly after our first meeting. Margarita found her a doctor who will treat her at a reduced fee, and even after I leave Flint, Margarita still sends me periodic updates about Lilliana. She takes Lilliana to the hospital one day and then texts me to say her nausea is so bad, she is thinking of stopping treatment. I text Lilliana photographs of beautiful birds to cheer her up: the hyacinth macaw, a black-billed bluebird with yellow-black eyes, a wood duck and a cute yellow duckling, an Atlantic puffin with its stupid face, the golden pheasant and its hillbilly yellow 'do, the red macaw, classic Amazonian prince. I keep texting birds but don't hear back.

Later I dream that the hawks started coming after she loses her hair from the chemo. Outside her house, the usual yard birds gather, drawn by the feeders filled with seed Lilliana placed out there and the big mature trees surrounding her home. The first time it happens she sees a raptor snatch a mourning dove and fly off with it. It makes her sick and she goes back inside. Then she sees it happen again. This time it is a cardinal and the raptor goes up to her roof to take plunder in its organs. Lilliana keeps going outside every day for stretches of time because it helps with her nausea and that's when she starts seeing hawks flying overhead. They are different sizes. They don't look like they could carry dogs and cats like her neighbors were saying, but they do look like they could kill. Soon they begin circling above where she stands to watch them from her yard, and when she stands beneath them, with some fear, to observe their majesty, she becomes certain that her limbs are tied to their wings with string, like a puppeteer's, and that she can control their movement. They are migratory birds. *Perhaps they had gotten lost, and she needed to guide them to warmth,* she thought. They'd die if she did not precipitate their movement with her movement, with the movement of flight. She needed to leave this house, this sickness. She feels ill in her heart because she could not leave the house, so the raptors form nests in the large mature trees surrounding the house and they've been there all this while, flying above her in whatever way she moves that day, to hunt or to take shits on her husband when he comes home at night.

You have already met Theodoro, but he was quiet before, so you did not notice him. He was one of the immigrants I met with in the church auditorium after mass. I had tried to make a lot of eye contact with him when he spoke because as soon as someone interrupted him, he shut down and looked pained. Theodoro is a lonely, ancient man, but he says he is fifty-six. He is a tree. His mouth is curved downward, wrinkles set deep like bark grooves, and he looks even older when he smiles. We talk on the phone late at night, after he's home from work, and our conversations feel like dark, hardened sap.

Theodoro came to the United States on August 20, 1998. He remembers the exact date. That was two years after his fifteen-year-old son first came north to go work at a top Chinese restaurant in Michigan that he heard, through friends, was hiring. First Theodoro worked at a cucumber plant, then in restaurants as a dishwasher and a cook, then in various factories: making Volkswagens, weapons, dishwashers, plastics, and soap.

But his favorite place to work was at a chocolate and sweets factory in Detroit, where he spent ten years. He started out cleaning bathrooms, but the couple who owned the factory saw that he was a good worker and said, *Theodoro, leave that alone. You can go work in the granola station now,* so he put on a blue lab coat and became a sweets man.

"My years at the chocolate factory were the most beautiful time of my life," Theodoro tells me. He learned how to make caramel-covered popcorn, pecan pies, cherry-center bonbons, little chocolate turtles with nuts inside. The aromas, of course, were incredible, but what he loved most were the machines. "At the start of the assembly line, I mixed in honey with the peanuts, then saw them go into the chocolate machine where chocolate cascaded down like a curtain but also up like a geyser; it showered chocolate from both directions, if you can imagine that. Now, at this point the chocolate was very hot, and it went into a cooling tunnel. There were times when I worked the night shift to make chocolate overnight, and the factory was quiet and cold, a few people making sweets for the world. I was very good at my job and I helped everyone around me, even though my supervisor said, *That's not your job.* But I wanted us to work as a team, so if I had a second, and my co-workers were slowing down, I ignored him. The last year I was there, they got these really old ovens that toasted the granola for a really long time and out it came, toasted and brown, smelling like heaven, and you had ten people working on eighty trays at a time. There were metal detectors in the cooling station, to make sure the batch was clean. It smelled like paradise. When I talk about it, it sounds impossible, but I saw it happen."

Then the company was sold to an owner from Ohio who was going to hire only American citizens. Theodoro's bosses broke the news to him on New Year's Day 2012. "I had been working for just about two hours and they sent for me. *Theodoro,* they said, *we can't keep you here. This company isn't ours anymore."* They gave him a certificate saying he was one of the best employees they'd ever had, and they hoped that when he showed it to future employers he wouldn't have to wash bathrooms anymore.

"Did they say that to you?" I ask.

"They really did," he says.

He lives alone in a house he purchased in 2009—cash. I ask him how it feels to be alone. "Sometimes I think of sad things, but I need to be in a good mood, so I put myself in a good mood," he says.

"Why do you have to be in a good mood?" I ask him.

"So I don't feel lonely."

He lives with his two pit bulls, Gracie and Bella. Gracie is a two-year-old blond pup and Bella is her six-year-old mom. He calls them both "the puppies." After rescuing them, he swung by a local mechanic to buy a large wooden doghouse to put in his yard. The dogs play outside for hours every day, get muddy, then need to be bathed. Gracie prefers to be bathed in very hot water, and when he is soaping her up, she is so comfortable that she'll fall asleep in the tub and has to be carried out in a towel, her limbs heavy, a truly spoiled creature.

I picture Theodoro hanging a tire from a tree in his back-yard, where he sits with Gracie and Bella on his lap and he swings with them, at first his feet barely off the ground, then higher and faster until he feels that if he falls, they will fall with him, and if one of them falls, he will fall with them, one body in motion just as they move alone in their house, alone in their yard, alone in all of Michigan, with not a soul in the world who loves them more than they love one another.

I ask Theodoro whether he gives Gracie and Bella tap water.

"No. I always give them water from the little water bottles they donate to us here in Flint," he says. He gives from his ra-tions.

Theodoro did not hear about the lead in the water until it made the international news. "When you're undocumented, you're the last to know," he says. He went to distribution cen-ters but they asked Theodoro for a state ID. He does not have a state ID, which undocumented immigrants are currently barred from having in Michigan, so he kept going to other sites until he could get water without an ID—he needed the water for his dogs. Men in uniform helped him put cases of bottled water in his car trunk, and he tells me this with a tone of admiration; he fears the National Guard but is also in awe of them.

I am lonely, too. I only feel peace with my puppy mill dog. When I got him, it was the week of Trump's inauguration and I was watching videos of black labs and German shepherds helping veterans with PTSD, jumping up at their faces when they were crying, shielding their bodies with their own, and I just cried into a pillow, wanting to be protected. I was super suicidal, and one night my partner was just like, you've never even been around a puppy. So we went into a pet shop just to play with a dog—look, we tried rescues, they denied us because we didn't have a yard—to distract me for long enough to stop me from slitting my wrists, and they brought out Frank. He's a Boston Terrier. A brown one. A really fucked-up-looking one. His eye was busted. He couldn't walk. My partner held him and deposited him into my lap and he fell asleep immediately, and when I got up because my leg fell asleep he bit at my pant leg and demanded I go back down on the floor, and I looked up at her and said, well, we can't leave him here. I hadn't gotten my book advance yet, so we took him out on layaway. Fucking shady shit. We took him home, and put him in his crate, and in the middle of the night I had a panic attack and we brought him out and put him on my chest and for the first time in my life I felt safe. He smelled like an unsullied childhood. He smelled like a baby without a childhood. He smelled like god had made an exception for me. So long as I kept myself alive to keep him alive, we'd be all right.

So when Theodoro tells me he gives his own rations of filtered water to the dogs, I feel like dying, but the kind of death that rebirths you into something less painful, like a tree, a tree like him. I ask him to text me pictures of his pit bulls and he sends them to me. They're plump. Their coats are shiny. Why do you give them your own water, I ask him. Well, they can't really speak, but if they could speak, they'd have a lot to say, he tells me.

♦ ♦ ♦

I come back to Flint almost a year later, after Governor Rick Snyder announces that the state of Michigan will stop providing free water to Flint residents because lead levels have not exceeded federal limits in two years, even though they've replaced only sixty-two hundred pipes affected by lead and have about twelve thousand to go. In addition to the high water bills they have to pay to the city that poisoned them, they will now have to buy their own clean water.

Margarita is thrilled that I have returned and hosts me at her home, where she has invited several immigrant women from Flint over for lunch to talk to me. For the special occasion, she has made tortillas from scratch, rice, and ground beef with potatoes. But the women never show for various reasons, some of them unconvincingly disguising their discomfort with the idea of talking to a stranger from New York, so instead, I meet Margarita's husband, Kenny, a tough guy with a tough-guy demeanor, who keeps telling her to slow down and take it easy. She's full of ideas for the community and she helps everyone, he says. Kenny did some time in prison, ten years, made some bad decisions. He hates cops. Calls them pigs. Kenny tells me the plot of *Serpico*, an Al Pacino movie about corruption among police; so, at some point Pacino's character gets shot in the face during a drug sting, and Kenny says it's based on a true story.

"Baby, it's not based on a true story," Margarita says.

"Hell yeah, it's based on a true story," Kenny says.

"You think everything is based on a true story," Margarita says.

"A lot of movies *are* based on true stories," Kenny says.

In Kenny's own story, the one about his life, it was a Latinx cop who infiltrated his friend group, got close to him, and pushed him to do certain things that resulted in his arrest—by the same Latinx cop. At the court hearing, Kenny's mother scolded the cop. "You're a traitor to your own people," she said. "It's my job," he told her. "I was just following orders."

The next day, Margarita introduces me to her friend Salma Pinzón. We meet at the Sloan Museum in the Flint Cultural Center, which is a museum dedicated to the history of Flint, with a particular focus on the rise and fall of the automobile industry. She's been there many times. It's my first. The water fountains in the museum have signs above them that say PLEASE DO NOT USE WATER FOUNTAIN. HELP YOURSELF TO THE COMPLIMEN-TARY WATER COOLER. The exhibits include miniatures of town buildings, collections of guns and pistols, union jackets, a mural dedicated to a United Auto Workers Labor Day Picnic, and an expansive re-creation, with life-size mannequins, of the Flint Sit-Down Strike, where the mothers and wives of the striking autoworkers broke windows in the factories to allow their men to breathe after they were teargassed by police. There are assembly-line station games where you are timed to perform assembly-line tasks; a loud bell sounds if you fail. Salma is good at that game.

Salma Pinzón has a date in immigration court. I ask her if she has her outfit planned. She doesn't. But I've had her outfit planned since she told me she has a court date.

Her hero is the late Mexican American singer Jenni Rivera

(1969–2012), a charismatic, voluptuous terror of a woman whose song "Sin Capitán" is Salma's favorite. Some lyrics: *My boat doesn't need a captain / because I've conquered the storm alone.*

"I think I'm just like her," Salma says.

The dress I have in mind for her to wear to immigration court is something Jenni had worn for the Latin Grammys in 2010. A gown. Royal purple with bell sleeves, with a deep V-cut, tight at the chest, bodice, and hips, then ruffled out accordion-style, with the smallest layers at the front. Yellow marigolds embroidered on the dress, and a marigold yellow shawl to wear around her shoulders. Salma's hair is long, waist-length, black everywhere but the crown, where it is white, but she has two months to begin bleaching it. She will be blond for the court date. Not a flattering, buttery warm blond, no—cold, ice blond. It won't look great but it'll be striking, and I'd rather she look striking than pretty.

Salma has a son with autism, Felipe, who is twenty-three years old now. He was eligible for DACA but she didn't sign him up out of fear that his information was going to be used against him. He doesn't speak Spanish, and she lives in fear that he'll be deported. What would he do in Mexico? "People over there would be cruel with kids like him," she says.

Salma has a date at immigration court because an ICE officer followed her around looking for a reason to arrest her. She said she protested and it was fruitless.

He took her to a detention center. She was detained for a month, alongside women with theft and drug charges, all of whom complained that they thought she had been unfairly de-tained. She didn't have a lawyer then and she doesn't have a lawyer now. No one has wanted to take on her case. She's making phone calls. She begins to cry and admits she doesn't have much hope but doesn't know what will happen to her son.

"I don't know what's going to happen at my court date. I don't know what god wants." But I know what god wants. God wants to see her in the motherfucking gown, unrepentant, with no captain.

Ivy was born in Mexico to a father who is an American citizen and a mother who is Mexican. After their divorce, her father won the custody battle so she came to Texas to live with him when she was eleven, and moved to Flint after he bought a house there on eBay in 2009. She is a single mom. She had a baby, Lidia, when she was twenty-one. During her pregnancy, which was during the water crisis, doctors responded to any health concerns she had by telling her to drink more water. "I would tell them I had fever and vomiting and they kept saying I needed to drink more water, everything was me needing to lay off the Coke and drink more water; it was a constant dismissal. But I didn't have money for anything other than tap water so that's what I drank."

I meet Ivy and her baby at a break during a Latino Leaders meeting one morning. It's a group of mostly Mexican American members of the Flint community with personal business cards and fantastic border accents who want to make the city more hospitable for Latinx and especially immigrant members. The meeting is conducted in English. Ivy takes notes during the meeting, and raises her hand to say something brilliant. The others nod and take notes. Her father shushes the baby in the other room. At eleven o'clock, they call a break for assemble-your-own taco bowls. Ivy comes over to me and writes down her number, angrily, in my notebook. She is pissed. She wants to talk. She is also young, really young, and has a full-moon face and long, straight black hair that she wears with a center part. I try to engage with the baby. I tell the one-year-old baby that it is good she is bilingual.

Ivy remembers, in vivid detail, the day she realized the water was dirty. "I remember taking a shower one day, and when I ran my hand over my skin there was a sticky layer all over my body that hadn't washed off. It was like jelly. I felt dirty. My neighbor brought a water jug to our house wanting to know if our water was like hers. It was yellow with some brown film in it. Yet we got letters from the city saying it was fine, that they were taking care of it. So what can you do?"

Ivy developed hives and rashes, for which she was prescribed steroids while she was pregnant. The doctors never performed any tests to determine the origin of the skin irritations. Then her baby girl was born. Over time, Ivy noticed the baby did not react to her or to motion, crying constantly and piercingly as if she was in tremendous fear, and when she took her to the doctor, he told her they'd just have to wait and see. "They did the exam and said we were going to have to give it a couple of months. A waiting game."

The doctor waited four months before determining the baby was blind from the lead poisoning.

"Her first seizure was when she was three months old. I always put her in her own bed at night, but for some reason, on this one particular night I brought her over to sleep with me, and all of a sudden I saw her shaking violently in a terrifying way. I picked her up, screaming, and ran her to my father. I have never felt such regret or guilt. They say breastfeeding is the safest, best thing you can do for your child, but it was after the fact that they said that if you have lead in your body and you breastfeed, you pass it on. When I heard that, my heart just dropped. I don't know if it happened when she was in my womb or after. If she has any delays or any problems down the line, I couldn't begin to apologize to her enough. I feel so much guilt."

Ivy's baby has regained her vision, but nobody knows what the long-term effects of the water poisoning will be in her little body. The wait is torturous for Ivy. It is torturous for her mom. It is torturous for the community. It is not torturous for the government. They want us all dead, Latinxs, black people, they want us dead, and sometimes they'll slip something into our bloodstreams to kill us slowly and sometimes they'll shoot and shoot and shoot and shoot and shoot shoot and shoot and shoot and shoot and shoot shoot and shoot and shoot and shoot shoot and shoot and shoot and shoot and shoot shoot and shoot and shoot and shoot and shoot shoot and shoot and shoot and shoot and shoot and shoot shoot and shoot and shoot and shoot shoot and shoot and shoot and shoot and shoot shoot and shoot and shoot and shoot and shoot shoot and shoot until their bloodlust is satisfied and it's all the same, our pastors will say god has a plan for us and our parents will plead with the Lord until the end to give them an answer.

I am not a journalist. Journalists are not allowed to get *involved* the way I have gotten involved. Journalists, to the best of my knowledge, do not try to change the outcome of their stories as crudely as I do. I send water. I fight with immigration lawyers. I raise money. I make arrangements with supernatural spirits to stop deportations. I try to solve shit the way an immigrant's kids try to solve shit for their parent because these people are all my parents, I am their child, if I wasn't their child—and I was their child—I should be patented and mass-produced and distributed to undocumented immigrants at Walmarts. I am a professional immigrant's daughter. My job was simple, to tell this story: The government wanted the people of Flint dead, or did not care if they died, which is the same thing, and set in motion a plan for them to be killed slowly through negligence at the highest levels. What I saw in Flint was a microcosm of the way the government treats the undocumented everywhere, making the conditions in this country as deadly and toxic and inhumane as possible so that we will self-deport. What I saw in Flint was what I had seen everywhere else, what I had felt in my own poisoned blood and bones. Being killed softly, silently, and with impunity.

The whitest thing I have ever done in my life was not repeatedly trying to get bangs after seeing pictures of Zooey Deschanel. The whitest thing I've done in my life was trying to save Flint youth while I was visiting there. At various points when I was in Flint, I did a cowardly thing, which was to try to suggest a trip in which some of the kids would come to New York with me, because I wanted to open a Pandora's box for them, the view of the city at night. The skyline! The fucking skyline! I asked the teens if they'd seen New York (they hadn't), and then asked them if they'd like to see New York (they didn't know), and holy fuck I hadn't anticipated that. In my mind, the kids would want to get out. They'd have big Broadway dreams. They'd have questions, they'd want *answers*, we'd talk gypsy cabs and SAT scores and Plan B both in life and in birth control.

But what happened instead is that the teens conscientiously ignored me the entire time I was there—they had no intention of
talking to me—so I'd eavesdrop on their conversations, and I'd
overhear them talking about how they wanted to be waitresses
at some local bar because they heard you could earn mad tips
that way, and I fucking DIED, because I grew up on my dad's
tips and knew what kind of life that gave you, and I wanted to
save them from that. I'd drunk the social mobility Kool-Aid
from college prep programs run by white people when I was in
high school and didn't know how to reconcile all that with what
I was seeing in Flint. I had created for myself a world in which
I could only feel reprieve from panic if my parents were either
dead or at peace, preferably both, and if they were to be just at
peace, that would be expensive, and I had to work toward that,
and I knew to the gram just how much blood they had shed for
me over the past thirty years and I had to repay it in gold. And
I didn't understand these kids who didn't think the same way. I
felt like it was our one fucking job—they were alien to me. I
didn't know how to talk to them. So I didn't.

When Margarita and I drove around the city, I asked her if
she had any kids in mind whom I could help write college entrance essays and she said no and I insisted and she said no, she
couldn't think of any, and I said, *Oh, okay, cool cool cool.*

On the third day of my first visit in Flint, I texted my friend
Max who has a pill problem and I told him I was thinking of
drinking the water and he definitely told me not to and I said,
*I know I know but I feel so guilty, and maybe I'd feel less guilty if I just
drank the fucking water.* Then I felt like I sounded like a white
girl trying to slum it, so that made me feel disgusted with myself, so now I felt like cutting my arm with the room service

knife but that seemed even whiter, so I didn't do anything at all, I just went to my hotel, where they gave us free water bottles for everything, even for brushing our teeth, and where there was a machine on the first floor for guests to refill their reusable water bottles and the TV on the first floor was always on Fox News even though the manager was black and he always smiled at me in the mornings when I went to get coffee, not knowing I was a bad girl in a good city, in a country that wanted both of us dead.

CHAPTER 5

Cleveland

S trictly as a matter of taste, I do not like children. Small animals are adorable in the way my biology programs me to find large-eyed, small-skulled mammals adorable, and they can grow up into formidable or admirable creatures—cubs become bears, calves become elephants, fledglings become eagles. Babies lack language, which makes me bored and impatient, then turn into children, whose saccharine vocal emissions grate my nerves, and then turn into adult humans, the most monstrous of all animals. But kids do not do the kinds of things adults are capable of that earn them some goodwill with me—like breed the French bulldog, perform open-heart surgery, tell good jokes. In general, kids don't mind me, because I leave them alone. I respect them. *How do you do*, I say. *Terrible*, they say. We're good.

But then, when I see a video online of three small boys, all American citizens, saying goodbye to their father at Cleveland Hopkins International Airport as he is being deported, my heart stops. They remind me of my brother. Meaning: They are boys, they are skinny and brown, they have heads of thick, jet-black hair for which there does not exist a single good haircut. I am ten years older than my brother, a mentor but not quite a mother figure, more like Gandalf to the hobbits, and this video awakens in me a lion's heart of desire to protect. I contact their lawyer. I want to help these children, I say. I want to become their role model. Do they like dogs? I write the boys a letter through their lawyer. "The first generation of immigrants comes to this country to work hard, and they often suffer and are treated badly. Do you know why they do it? For their children. That's us. It's up to us to honor our parents' sacrifices by doing better than they did, by having better lives than what we saw growing up. I'm here to tell you that the best way to do that is through an education," I write. I'm brainwashed.

A couple of months later, I travel to Willard, Ohio, to meet them. Willard is the most rural place I have ever been to, and on the long drive there I pass through vast stretches of farmland where my cheap cell phone loses service completely. Willard is known for its rich, fertile soil—people call it "the muck"—and its agricultural industry is booming, which means that tempo-rary workers from Mexico come in seasonally to help plant, weed, and harvest. Before I visited Willard, there was a huge battle over a welcome-home party that the chamber of com-merce was throwing the migrant workers. A Vietnam War vet threw a tantrum in a letter to the editor of the local newspaper, writing, "Myself and a lot of other Vietnam veterans and also Korean veterans are still waiting on our welcome-home party. Where does the Willard City Chamber of Commerce think that it is right to give the migrant workers a welcome back party?"

At a city meeting dedicated to planning the party, a woman stormed out of the room with her husband, saying, "I'm a compassionate person. I believe people who come here have to come here the right way. It makes me angry when I hear people talking about harboring illegals." The city has a population of approximately six thousand people, 94 percent of whom are white. This is where the boys live.

I come armed with the cutest pictures of my dog back when he was a puppy because I assume all children like puppies. When I arrive, I find out three of the four children are scared of dogs. (There are three boys and an even smaller child, a girl.) And clowns. I could not have arrived at a better time. They want to discuss their fear of clowns.

They have been having nightmares of clowns. They have been watching horror movies because they are spending a lot of unsupervised time at home because their mother is working long hours to support them now that their household has only a single income. They tell me about a YouTube video they watched where a drone flying over a field shows a clown with a machete ready to kill children. Andres is fourteen, Omar is eleven, Elias is ten, and Greta is six. "You don't understand, they kill you with machetes," says Omar. In English, *MACH-eh-teh* is pronounced *mah-SHEH-tee*, I say. "They kill you with *ma-SHEH-tees*," they say.

The video is called *Hunting Killer Clowns with Drone! We Found One! (Not Clickbait!)* and it is made by two preteen boys who fly a drone over a field, out of which jumps a tall person in white face paint and a toy machete. The boys are not good actors, the machete does not look real, and it is not believable in the slightest. Jesus Christ, I think. These are *children.*

Javier Quintanilla, their dad, had lived in the United States for sixteen years. He was stopped for driving without a license in 2008, and local police alerted ICE. After a deportation order was issued in 2011, he was granted a stay to remain in the country, and he dutifully checked in with immigration authorities every six months until March of 2017, when an immigration agent met him at his appointment and told him to get ready to be deported.

In the weeks leading up to his deportation, Javier and the kids went door-to-door around Willard asking their neighbors to sign a petition asking for his stay. (Courts sometimes consider community support in deciding whether someone gets a stay, and it helps mobilize support for the case.) Not everyone was nice to them. It was fruitless. When the day came, Javier did not even pack a bag, just a folder of his immigration documents. He thought something or someone was going to intervene at the last moment. "We went to the airport but we had hope until the very end," his wife, Patricia, says. When they said goodbye, Javier told her he loved her and made her promise she'd take good care of the children. He, in turn, promised he would come back. When Patricia and the kids returned home, the house still smelled like him. His sneakers were lying on the floor, his dirty clothes were in the hamper, his toothbrush was in the bathroom, not yet dry from that morning. His razor sat in the shower. It would soon begin to rust. He was everywhere and he was gone.

Both sides have adhered to the promise to talk on the phone every day, but Javier is different now. The trauma of being separated from his family and being forcefully removed like a criminal has worn at his mental health. It started even before he left. As the date of his deportation approached, he became short-tempered and silent. His ankle monitor had only an eight-hour charge, so he had to charge it while he was at work, which was humiliating. Patricia often tripped over the ankle monitor charger. "He's a changed man," she says. "He wants to express himself and tell us that he misses us, but for some reason he can't. He says, *I can't see you, I don't know what you're doing,* and it frustrates him. He's impatient, he's mad all the time, he's moody all the time."

Peter Maximillian, the family's immigration lawyer, has made an impression on the children, who are hungry for male protection. He dresses well and has his own office, which the children think is incredible. He is the most powerful person they know. Andres is especially besotted. Peter comes down from Cleveland on a Saturday to take the children to lunch with me. They want to go to Applebee's, which is forty-five minutes away, and Patricia asks me to please make sure they don't smother Peter, which I quickly see they are keen on doing. We end up going to Wendy's instead, because it's only about five minutes away. Andres says he wants them to make an exception of their minimum age requirement—sixteen—so he can work there. He is fourteen. "I'm the man of the house now," he says in the back seat of the car, and Greta punches him. When Javier left, so did the only member of the family who drove. Now they are stuck in rural Ohio without a car. Andres walks three miles to the grocery store and returns carrying heavy bags. He was going to join the wrestling team but now has to come home right after school to take care of his younger siblings. He watches them while their mother is at work. Patricia sometimes takes an English class after work, and comes home in the evening. She is always tired, and when she gets home, she cleans, cooks, and sits on the couch, running her fingers through Greta's hair while she draws, her eyes fixed on a point in the middle of the room, barely blinking.

About a week after returning to Connecticut, I am in the shower and get a call from the boys. Omar is doing his science homework and wants to get an A on it. He says he has a question: Do trees die during the winter?

I begin to improvise, summoning forth everything I know about winter, about plants, about death, about Holden Caulfield asking the exact same question about ducks in Central Park, about how old the kids will have to be before I can explain to them what *allusions* are, about how I still think knowing what allusions are can save them. My partner whispers: *Look. It. Up.*

How do trees survive in winter? Omar asks me. It seems like they should die. How can they live without the sun? I wrap a towel around myself and run to my computer. "Trees go through a process similar to hibernation called dormancy, and that is what keeps them alive during the winter," I read from the screen. Do you know what dormancy means? It comes from the Spanish word dormir, "to sleep," I lie. Isn't that cool? I ask. They sleep right through the winter, and when they wake up, it is spring again.

Javier used to work at a factory packing cookies. He would often bring home small cheddar crackers in the shape of goldfish. Those were their favorite. Andres is not his biological child. Patricia had him young, when she was eighteen. Andres was a year old when she got together with Javier, who cared for him like they shared blood. She always thought there was something special about the way Javier took care of Andres. "He's just given him more than the others. Everything Andres has wanted he has always received." Because they were always family, and because they thought the adoption process would be overly complicated and expensive, they kept putting off a formal adoption. But as the boys got older and began asking why they did not all share the same last name, it became clear that Javier would adopt Andres. So a couple of years ago, they went in front of a judge, who told Patricia she liked to ask the same question to everyone who went in front of her with an adoption request. "Tell me one thing that's going to make me sign this order."

"He doesn't know another father," Patricia responded. "Javier used to work the night shift so he was always with the boys during the day and he took care of Andres from the time he was a baby. He bathed him, he always changed his diaper." "I've heard enough," Patricia remembers the judge saying. The family celebrated that night. Every evening, before Javier began his shift, they would all sit together after dinner to drink coffee, talk, and watch the evening news. They were news junkies and kept each other close. "Even if it was to put gas in the car, all six of us went."

Patricia is small, with heart-shaped purple lips and black hair pulled back into an elegant knot. When I met her, she was wearing purple acrylic nails on one hand and short nails filed in a round shape on the other. She wears glasses with clear rectangular lenses and modest, nondescript clothing in dark colors. She speaks to me warmly in a conspiratorial whisper, especially in the presence of Peter, the lawyer, who does not speak Spanish. She giggles as she observes the boys crowding over where he is sitting, showing him funny videos on their phone. *Look at them. He's going to walk out! He's going to explode! He can't put up with them!* I wonder how she was with Javier, with her sidekick

laugh and expressive almond-shaped eyes. I wonder what se-
crets they kept together, what inside jokes made them laugh,
before they were separated and it all turned sour.

Omar is skinny, with a top lip that looks carved in amethyst.
His mom tells me he is a solitary soul, and while the entire family crowds the living room during my visit, he is not there. He's
up in his room a lot. When we go out to Wendy's, he picks a
two-person table across from us and sits alone. I call him over to
sit next to me. He asks how old I am and I tell him to guess. He
guesses nineteen—a hopeful guess because he has a crush on
me. I tell him I am old enough to be his mother, and he blushes.

"Omar does not cry," Patricia tells me. "He has not cried once.
He is stoic and strong, but he is the one who asks after his father
the most." Classmates have been taunting him at school. "I hope
your mom gets sent back to Mexico too," they tell him. I ask
him how he is sleeping, and he says that he tells himself his dad
will be gone for only a few weeks. "Last night, I did not sleep at
all because I missed my dad." So he tucked himself into his
mother's bed. I have brought him a copy of the first book in the
Diary of a Wimpy Kid series, on my brother's recommendation.
A lucky guess. Turns out Omar loves the series and has taken
the books out of his local library. He's never owned a copy of his
own. Omar asks me to sign the book because although I am not
its author, I am *an* author, and he thinks that's pretty cool. I
autograph it.

In the pictures of the scene at the airport, moments before
Javier was deported, the only one photographed crying is Elias.
He is ten years old. Elias says he misses going to the mall with
his dad, where he would spoil him and buy him treats, and he
misses how his dad would make funny voices to make him laugh,

like the impression he made of the old-timey children's character El Chavo, a grown actor assuming the voice of a child.
"Sometimes I dream the world is going to crack open and I am
going to fall inside," he says. While I am talking to his mother,
Elias goes upstairs to bring down his report card to show me.
Some Bs and Cs in the humanities but a perfect 100 in math. He
says his favorite way of passing the time is by doing multiplica-
tion exercises with decimals in his head. After I return to Connecticut, Elias texts me formal greetings and terrible pictures
of himself with the camera lens pointing up. One early morning
he sends me a picture of Greta all dressed up, wearing a long
white tulle skirt and a denim vest with a doily collar. She is
wearing a tight ponytail and doing ballerina poses. He sends
them at 7:24 in the morning. I wonder if he just thought his
sister looked pretty but had no one to share it with. *Good morning Karla. How are you today?*

Greta is a terror. She laughs hysterically—she cackles—at
her own jokes, and she ranks her brothers in order of how much
she hates them, which is actually the order of how much she
loves them, and punches the winner, usually Andres. She spends
the entire time drawing and hangs up the drawings on the wall
herself, then puts her hand under her chin like an art critic and
makes exclamations about the drawing. She steals her brothers'
cell phone to send text messages to Patricia about how much
she loves her, even when she is sitting on the same couch or in
the adjacent room. Sometimes she sends me a long, multiline
string of emojis that she signs *Greta*. I brought her a tiny pink
plush purse carrying a plush puppy. If god is fair, he will allow
her to grow up into a woman with the resources to spoil a stupid toy breed like a Cavapoo that she'll carry around in a purse.

Patricia tells me Greta stopped eating after her father left, and lost a lot of weight. When I visit, she barely touches her food.

Stories in the news often end at the deportation, at the airport scene. But each deportation means a shattered family, a marriage ending, a custody battle, children who overnight go from being raised by two parents to one parent with a single income, children who become orphans in foster care. One study found that family income dropped around 70 percent after a deportation. Another study found that American-citizen children born to immigrant parents who were detained or deported suffered greater rates of PTSD than their peers. I know Javier wants the children to move to Mexico to be with him, and it is a source of fights with Patricia. "I think it's selfish to take the children to Mexico," she says. "This is their country. The whole point was to allow them to receive an education here." A coffee plantation awaits them in Mexico. But even if they stay in Ohio, things look bleak.

The boys are worried about winter coming for the first time without their father in the house. They have no car. They are in the middle of rural Ohio. Everything is so far away. Andres, who will start high school next fall, walks a few miles down to the local public library to do his homework when he needs a computer, but with winter coming, it gets dark early. I have a fundraiser among my friends and collect enough money to buy the family a used MacBook and a year's worth of Internet. That's a thing I do sometimes—hold fundraisers among people I know for migrants I love who are in need. It's the same people who donate every time, older white hippies and children of immigrants, not my former Harvard classmates who post pictures of themselves at rooftop happy hours every day, the kids who work at Silicon Valley start-ups, the ones who have precious weddings with hashtags and babies they want to make sure you know the sex of. At night, at around 8:00 P.M., when I decide that I want the day to be over and close all the blinds because it's time to usher in unconsciousness, in the delicious few seconds before sleep befalls me, I imagine them being fatally impaled by a stop sign on a trip abroad.

Anyway, I write down a list of rules for the boys. I write them a card. I set up the password to their computer. It is *studyhard*. I tell them that school got me out, that it can get them out. *Out.* Out of what? The ghetto? I grew up poorer than I remember. But I grew up with two parents. I grew up with nightmares but they are living through nightmares.

I am almost six hundred miles away. I'd never seen a tractor before I visited them, and they've never seen New York. There are no clowns in fields with machetes in America. There are white moms who threw stones at the little girls in Little Rock and there are white moms who wish Andres and Omar and Elias and Greta's mom will be deported too. There are no clowns in fields with machetes, but there are ICE officers who pose as nice people trying to buy a piñata off the Internet, meet you in a parking lot, and detain you. *If we get good grades, will you take us to New York City? Is Connecticut near Cleveland? What's the best college in the whole country? I'm going to go to Harvard. I'll become an immigration lawyer, like Peter, so nobody's dad will ever be taken away again.*

I start my days sitting on the floor of my shower, naked, the water as hot as I can bear it blasting onto my head. I find relief only in the water. For the past ten days, I've had a migraine that follows me like a shadow. One hundred and forty-two hours of incessant pain, an eight on the ten-point scale. My doctor has suggested codeine, which I refused, because once I took too much Percocet after a tooth extraction and threw up for twenty-four hours straight. I have a CT scan, an MRI, I go to the neurologist—the readings are all inconclusive. I'm told it's a migraine with an unknown cause. *Have you tried yoga?* they say.

"Stress headache," says Leonel Chávez when I visit him one morning. Leonel is a forty-five-year-old Ecuadorian man holed up in a Methodist church off the Yale campus in defiance of ICE, which considers him a fugitive. He is in sanctuary. In 2007, a wrong turn during a family trip landed him in Canada and ICE took notice of him. A judge ordered his removal in 2009, but he managed to keep his head down and stay under the radar. In 2016, he was given a stay on the removal order as long as he checked in every six months. But under the current administration, the authorities have all but stopped granting stays, so in July 2017 he was ordered to leave within the month. Just like Javier. The day of his scheduled deportation, he claimed sanctuary in the church, a space that Immigration and Customs officers do not enter. He has been living in the church for over three months.

"Probably," I say. "But what can I do?"

He shoots me a look. "There's always something to be done," he says defiantly. "For example, me. I control my thoughts. I just move them away from what's causing me stress and onto something else. I've been doing that this entire time."

The migraine thing is new. I'll visit Leonel on a Monday, then wake up with a headache on a Tuesday and have to lie in the dark for the next two days, sometimes going to Urgent Care for a migraine cocktail through an IV. My arm starts looking like I use. Then I visit him again. The migraines will not stop. I will just have to start taking daily medication to prevent them and emergency medication at their onset. They will become a part of me, and Leonel will become a part of me, and the sanctuary movement will speak to me and my traumas in the way nothing ever has before.

Leonel arrived in Connecticut twenty years ago on a Sunday afternoon at two o'clock. A family friend's rotisserie-chicken restaurant was hiring a dishwasher. Dishwashing is a popular job for the newly arrived. It doesn't pay great, the hours are long, and it's boring and grueling, but Leonel was thrilled to see a job opportunity materialize so quickly after arriving. He took a shower and began his first work shift in America three hours after setting foot in the state. That's Leonel. Leonel is also handsome, like a cowboy. No, not like a cowboy. Like a bad boy with a toothpick in his mouth. Actually, no, forgive me, he is precisely the Ecuadorian version of Brad Pitt in *Inglourious Basterds*. A fine Nazi-killing small man.

Leonel has lived in the United States ever since and has firmly laid down roots. He left the restaurant industry and became an in-demand construction worker, which netted him a healthy income. His wife is named Sofía, and they have a daughter and a son in their twenties, both on DACA, who live with him in the house, as well as a twelve-year-old daughter, Diana, who was born in Connecticut and is an American citizen. She speaks to her parents in English. The older kids are busy with their jobs, but Diana visits her father in the church nearly every day after soccer practice. Diana is always hanging her body off her father lovingly, like a sloth on a tree. She loves dogs and has this really brilliant plan to travel to Ecuador to rescue street dogs and bring them to the United States to sell for profit, marked up for the Third World je ne sais quoi. I'm waiting until she turns eighteen to introduce her to venture capitalists. Sofía is consistently one of the most powerful speakers at rallies, vigils, and press conferences. She speaks off the cuff and brings everyone to tears. I am a little afraid of her because when she hugs me and looks at me, I feel like telling her I hurt too much.

As his time in sanctuary stretched from days to weeks to months, Leonel began to grow dark. "I am in a fight with myself all the time," he says. "I'm getting depressed more and more, I feel a desire to run out and leave this all behind. I ask the Lord that He not abandon me. On days I know I'm going to be alone, I don't want to wake up or even eat."

He has lost weight, and his hair, which he cut about two months into sanctuary, has grown back, curly and thick. He wears soft fabrics that fall loosely around his ankle monitor. Big sweatpants or shorts. He does not cry. "When I feel I am about to explode like a volcano, I'll watch sad movies or listen to sad songs, so then I cry to let it all out. But I'm crying about the movie or the song. I don't cry about this. They'll never have the pleasure of seeing me cry," he tells me. To occupy his mind, he built the church a modest but exquisite lectern with wood so thin it looks like paper, and a burgeoning cross in its center.

Welcoming an undocumented immigrant with a deportation order into a church has to be done carefully so it cannot be misconstrued as harboring a fugitive. As a first step, the church makes clear to ICE that they are acting within their capacity as a sanctuary space in accordance with their beliefs as followers of Jesus Christ. They send a fax to ICE headquarters announcing that the immigrant is there once he or she arrives so nobody can claim they are "hiding" them. All parties are aware of the immigrant's whereabouts. They're wearing ankle monitors given to them by the Florida private company GEO Group. Sanctuary works because ICE has a policy against forcing their way into places of worship. Violating that policy requires special permission from ICE headquarters, but so far that hasn't happened, and one immigration lawyer told me he thinks that if it did happen, "all hell would break loose." It would certainly be bad PR. The image of armed men in uniform forcing their way inside a church door being physically blocked by priests, rabbis, or imams is dramatic to think about, and although it hasn't happened, it feels imminent. The activists and religious leaders involved in the sanctuary movement think it's enough of a possibility that they have a plan for it. If ICE tries to force their way in, members of the congregation would rush to the church and try to block the door with their bodies.

In the United States, the tradition of immigrants claiming sanctuary in churches dates back to the 1980s, when a network of churches took in nearly five hundred thousand refugees fleeing the death squads in Central America. An underground railroad of sorts moved people through Mexico to more than five hundred places of worship across the country. After sending in undercover informants to infiltrate the movement, the federal government charged two Roman Catholic priests, a nun, and a Protestant minister with conspiracy to smuggle aliens, and they faced jail time of up to twenty-five years. They got probation instead.

But the tradition of sanctuary is even more ancient than that. In the Old Testament, Mosaic law determines that some cities should be set aside as "cities of refuge," where an individual who accidentally killed someone could be protected from prosecution. Saint Paul taught that any stranger who asked for help could be an angel undercover, and medieval churches would establish a range outside their walls within which refugees could not be arrested. There was an ancient Greek belief that someone turning away a supplicant ran the risk of turning away Zeus himself.

Leonel decided to go into sanctuary at the last minute. The first church the family approached denied them sanctuary because they wanted an assurance that the stay would be short, and Leonel and Sofía couldn't make that guarantee. "It was like your house is burning down and someone asks you for a month's rent first before lending you a hand," Leonel says. So they contacted Latinos Fighting for Justice, the local Latinx rights organization, which in turn reached out to Pastor Lisa at the Vineyard Church who welcomed Leonel, convinced that Jesus Christ would have done the same.

Leonel's room is upstairs; it used to be the pastor's office. His bed is in the corner, a twin bed low to the ground with thin, flat pillows and a crocheted brown blanket. The clock on the wall has been stuck at 12:22 for the past three months. It's like Vegas in this room: no windows anywhere and only a single broken clock. Small acrylic paintings of naturescapes line the walls, and I see Leonel has arranged an assortment of greeting cards on top of his air conditioner. There are shelves filled with cookies, chips, teas, and instant coffee. A small table and chairs in the middle of the room. One night family and local activists crowd into the room, sitting on the floor and on chairs and on his bed, and I ask Leonel what time he goes to sleep. "When the people leave," he says.

During one of my visits, I pull up a chair while Leonel is in the middle of telling his family about the South African photographer Kevin Carter and the picture he took of a large vulture approaching an emaciated toddler during the Sudanese famine. He scared the bird away but did not touch the child. It won the Pulitzer Prize in 1994. A few months later, Carter committed suicide. "That photo cost him his life," says Leonel. This anecdote comes up naturally during a discussion of starving children, which is part of a larger discussion of how fortunate we are in relation to the people all over the world who really *do* suffer. It's not hard to see why Leonel is intrigued by Kevin Carter. He doesn't understand how someone could visit a tragedy but not actively work to alleviate the suffering they witnessed. He doesn't understand how people could choose to watch a good man waste away in god's own house while the seasons continue their course and the church empties out of family each night, leaving him alone, with his thoughts, in the darkness. I don't say anything.

A lot happens while Leonel is in sanctuary—school shootings, daily bombshells in the special-counsel investigation of the president and his campaign—but I generally do not bring up the news with Leonel. I do not bring up the weather, even though that's the simplest way to start a conversation with another human being, remarking how cold or hot it is, how much it's raining. I shed my outer clothing as soon as I'm in the church

to try to hide the changing seasons from him. I try to wear basically the same thing. I do not want to cause him pain by reminding him of the outside world. I always contact him ahead of time
to plan my visits, and text him if I am running even five minutes
late. I notice that other visitors—old ladies from the church,
Yale kids—drop by unannounced, as if he were a man with
nothing but time to spare. We make hours go by with small talk.
I feel grief at the knowledge he's in there. I feel as if someone is
being killed and I am being forced to watch it, blinders on, and
the bullet travels in slow motion, but I cannot stop it.

Before I tell you what happens next, I should share with you
a little story about something I did when I was around fifteen
years old. My father was working as a deliveryman, and the
owner of the restaurant hired a new manager to oversee the
deliverymen—all immigrants, nearly all Mexican. The guy was
Puerto Rican—an American citizen—and became immediately
abusive, calling the delivery guys wetbacks and spics, threatening to call ICE on them, yelling at them, getting up in their
faces. My father fell into a bit of a depression. I had just watched
All the President's Men for the tenth time, and what I did was I
made myself a pot of tea, put on my best posh accent, dialed *69
to block my number, and called the restaurant. I asked to speak
to the owner. I said I was a beat reporter for a big city newspaper, and I had just received a tip from a customer about over-
hearing racist abuse in the kitchen and did he have a comment.
The owner said he'd handle it and asked me not to write the
story. *I don't know, man,* I said, *it's a pretty good story.* In the end,
the manager was fired, and the cloud over my father lifted. My
father was furious when I told him what I did, but not for a minute in the fourteen years since have I felt that what I did was

unethical, nor have I felt guilty for having a man fired. I'd do it again but my accent would be better.

So I got into a fight with Leonel's lawyer. I was working on a newspaper story on Leonel and he had been telling me for a long time that his lawyer had been treating him—communicating with him or not, mostly not—in ways I understood to be *negligent* and so I called him up and asked him a list of Bob Woodwardy questions that any discerning person would have understood meant I was asking around the issue of *negligence,* and he asked me to meet him at the church the following night at eight o'clock on the dot, like a playground bully, and yelled at me in front of Leonel and Sofía, told them they could not trust me, because he did not trust me, and they looked down at the floor because what could they say?—their lives were in his hands. So I was quiet for their sake, and also I am not a confrontational person— I am shy and I cry easily—and I went home and I cried and cried. But a few weeks later I sent him an expensive bottle of scotch to appease him because I needed to still have access to him, because access to him meant I could help Leonel. Our meeting forced him to go to the church for the first time in god knows how long, which is what Latinos Fighting for Justice had been trying to get him to do, and while he was there, they talked to him about a new strategy, which he agreed to pursue. One of the organizers called me that night to ask if I was okay and to say that never mind all that, the strategy had worked (oh yes, the strategy!). On Thanksgiving Day, out of nowhere, Leonel was released. He was out! He called me and I tried not to cry, because it wasn't about me, a known pussy, and our conversation was awkward. Are you stretching your legs, Leonel? Soon after, on Facebook, I saw a picture of him stepping outside the church for the first time while Sofía cried by his side and I am lucky I was already married and will not have kids so I do not have to lie about what the most beautiful thing I've ever seen is.

A few weeks later, my partner and I drive to Leonel and Sofía's home. He opens the door with his hair still wet from the shower. I tell him he looks great. "All that has changed is the location. I'm still a prisoner," he says, and points to his ankle bracelet. It's still on. A decision from the immigration courts can take hours or it can take months, maybe years. We admire his house, our first time seeing it. Then they get to the point— there is a new man who has just taken up sanctuary in a nearby church. His name is Francisco Valderrama. He is Ecuadorian too.

Most people with deportation orders do not go into sanctuary. Right now, there are only forty-two individuals in the United States living in churches in defiance of their deportation orders. It takes a particular kind of person to go into sanctuary. They're extraordinary.

From the undocumented people I have loved, I have learned that all of us share something a bit peculiar, fantastical, and controversial, which is this: We operate in this world like we are a little bit above the law. This does not mean we are not law-abiding. We have to be extremely careful not to have any run-ins with the law—because even a traffic ticket can lead to deportation. We pay taxes too. In 1996, the IRS even made a special provision for us to be able to pay taxes without Social Security numbers—that's the ITIN number, which you'll see advertised everywhere in immigrant neighborhoods.

But as an undocumented immigrant, everything we do is technically against the law. We're *illegal*. Many of us are indigenous in part or whole and do not believe borders should exist at all. I personally subscribe to Dr. King's definition of an "unjust law" as being "out of harmony with the moral law." And the higher moral law here is that people have a human right to move, to change location, if they experience hunger, poverty, violence, or lack of opportunity, especially if that climate in their home countries is created by the United States, as is the case with most third world countries from which people migrate. Ain't that 'bout a bitch?

Francisco Valderrama and Leonel Chávez have very specific profiles. They have young children and lives they love and do not want to give up. Still in their prime, they haven't been defeated by decades of racist abuse and manual labor yet; they walked into the church with their heads high. They're individuals of strong faith who do not lose hope easily. But they're also roguish. They're wild. They're stubborn. They're frontiersmen. They know how to make just about anything appear out of thin air, they have lovely homes they created from nothing but sheer will and obstinance, and when they were in trouble, they managed to find communities to rally around them. Francisco is a completely fluent English speaker whose leather couch and flatscreen TV are the result of him outsmarting big-box stores in perfectly legal but kind of eyebrow-raising ways. Now Francisco's home is an abandoned menagerie, a wildlife sanctuary cobwebbed by an apocalypse. His senior dog is alone most of the day, confused by why his dad disappeared one day. The two parakeets, Blue and Birdy, sing all day with nobody to hear their racket. A goldfish named Fishy swims in the dark.

Francisco's wife, Flor, is soft-spoken and shy and laughs easily, which hints to a private life their daughters have told us
about in which she is "extra" and "crazy." Their three American-
born children, Brianna, age sixteen, Franny, age thirteen, and
Johnny, age five, are also pretty extra. The girls are just like
Francisco: stubborn and overflowing with a restless energy.
Franny wants to become a famous actress "to prove white people wrong" and Brianna is a STEM whiz who wants to become
a nurse. Johnny, controversially, wants to be a cop. The children
visit their father at the church every day after school, and every
night when Johnny has to leave the church, to return to his fa-
therless home, he cries and that makes Francisco cry too.

I don't know how it happened. All I know is that at first, I
was resistant to meeting a new person in sanctuary because my
relationship with Leonel had made me sick, and the next thing
I knew, my partner and I were going over to the church for dinner with the family every week. Then more than once a week.
Francisco and Flor would cook some delicious folk Ecuadorian
dish to cure my newfound homesickness and it would feel like
going to bed with a hot water bottle. I would sometimes even
get warm and sleepy eating sopa de bola, a soup with green
plantains stuffed with meat, or encebollado, a warm tuna and
yucca soup that my partner ate a sixth of politely. We'd play a
game with the family, like Pictionary or charades, while all
wearing face masks, the skin-care kind, and it was easy. It was
never tense, there were no memories I had to work to suppress,
meaning it was like suddenly having the most loving and least
complicated family in the world, except that this family was in
hell. When I had my wisdom tooth removed, my partner had to
go to work, so she dropped me off at the church to recover and

I lay on the couch in the church basement, tucked in with blankets by Francisco, him sitting respectfully at the corner of the couch holding up an iPad for me to watch a documentary about the Inca Empire. Flor made me her special hen soup with a hen she had killed specially for me. My real family became extremely jealous. "They're taking advantage of you," my mother would text me, livid that I had spent yet another quiet evening with them, laughing and embracing, instead of talking to her. I told her to not talk to me about them again.

One night, we're having dinner with the Valderramas at the church and a religious group that Leonel and Sofía belong to stops by unannounced. Since leaving sanctuary, Leonel and Sofía have developed an unshakable concern for Francisco and his family. You can see it pains Leonel to visit, but the guilt of turning his back hurts more. They're about twenty people deep, and they bring guitars. They form a circle. Someone grabs my arm and brings me into the prayer circle. I sit between Leonel and Francisco. The first hour of the prayer session consists of the group of faithful men and women on their knees beating their chests and crying out to god for forgiveness. I look at them intently. Some of them seem for real but overall it's super performative. I do not pray to god for forgiveness, because I believe I have nothing to apologize for and he might have to explain a couple of things to *me*, so I just sit there, moping, angry, but still trying to radiate positive vibes because I'm not going to be the person who is ruining faithful migrants' experience of community. I respect the role of god in the lives of people who suffer but basically only in the lives of people who suffer.

One of the loudest chest beaters brings the two sanctuary couples to the center of the group. "We will pray for the families," she says, and then takes me by the hand too. "Oh, I'm not family," I say, but she shakes her head and says, "It doesn't matter. Jesus loves you." So we stand in the center of a prayer circle twenty people deep, and they say, *Close your eyes and hold hands.* I'm still in between Leonel and Francisco, so I hold on to their hands, tight. The two couples close their eyes and bow their heads. Prayer begins. As soon as the song starts, Francisco and Flor collapse into each other's arms. Tears fall onto Flor's baby-blue shirt. Leonel and I are not crying. We are still holding hands, fingers tightly interlaced, and we lock eyes. He guides my body so we wrap Francisco, Flor, and Sofía in our arms and squeeze.

When the prayer circle is done, I go back to my seat. I take advantage of a pause in the next round of prayers and walk out quietly. I go sit with Franny and Brianna in Francisco's room. When he sees me again, Leonel teases me. "Was the exorcism really hard on you, little atheist?"

Francisco's case moves slowly through the backlogged immigration courts. The months began to pass, quickly, slowly, marked only by legal dead ends and more prayer circles. My partner and I begin to play a larger and larger role in Franny and Brianna's lives. They begin to call us "moms." When we say we are going to pick them up for dinner at Buffalo Wild Wings, their favorite restaurant, basically all Connecticut teenagers' favorite restaurant, at six o'clock and it is 6:01, we receive a text message from Brianna: "It is 6:01." The girls decide that our friendship anniversary is on Brianna's birthday, which is February 23. That night, we took them to see *Black Panther* because I thought it would be inspiring for them as young women of color. I'm a didact. Franny texted throughout the whole thing and I was very upset! Within a few months, they were sleeping over. When February 23 rolled around for a second time, with their father still praying for a miracle, we decorated T-shirts with our friendship anniversary and hearts in glitter glue. There were times that Franny asked to come over to our apartment to do homework, so we picked her up from school, at enough of a distance from the entrance that we didn't embarrass her in front of the other tweens wearing spotless Air Force Ones, sat her at my desk, and pulled up a chair next to her to unsuccessfully remind her to bring down the X as she went through each step in an equation. We made sure she used the website that listed all answers for her textbook just to check her answers, not to cheat, and she relished the discipline. She enjoyed dangling provocations in front of us. *I'll cheat! I won't hand this in! I'll talk back to my teacher!* She was going to either do or not do those things anyway, but she liked it when we pleaded with her, gave her lectures on the importance of grades, and insisted on talking to her principal when she was treated unfairly by a teacher. Once, Franny said she didn't want to go to college and I said, "Oh hell yes you are," and told her I was going to take a needle and thread and sew her ear to mine so she would have to go wherever I went and I would go to college. She thought that was "crazy" and made me "a weirdo" but she enthusiastically repeated my words to her father, pleased I cared enough about her to put my ear through so much.

We were making dinner in the church basement one evening when Johnny suddenly asked his sister Brianna why their dad wasn't allowed to go home. He had long outgrown the original explanation, which was that his dad worked at the church, a special job with no time off. Brianna said there was an evil man who wasn't letting him leave. Johnny then turned to me and asked why the dinosaurs died. Johnny is obsessed with dinosaurs. He is as much an expert as a five-year-old can be. He knew why. But he wanted to hear me say it. So I told him that a meteor hit Earth and the dust blocked the sun and there was no food for the dinosaurs so the dinosaurs starved. "Yes," Johnny said empathically. The extinction of the dinosaurs is the only tragedy Johnny knows. He doesn't know about Hiroshima. He doesn't know about the Holocaust. He doesn't know about the Trail of Tears. He just knows his father can't come home and he knows the dinosaurs died.

When Francisco received news—not for the first time nor for the last—that his request for a stay was denied by local immigration authorities, faith leaders from around Connecticut set up an all-night prayer vigil outside the ICE offices in Hartford to plead with ICE to use its discretion to give Francisco a stay. They set up a table with pictures of Francisco with his children and tiny votive candles surrounding the frames. The pictures were from their life before—of the family at the park, fruit-picking, dressed for parties. Brianna stared at the pictures for a long time. "They made it look like Dad died," she whispered. Then she threw herself into the arms of my partner and sobbed. "When will this end?" she asked as she heaved. She could barely get out the words. When we all piled into the car and headed back to New Haven, the girls asked us to play sad music. An enormous yellow full moon followed our car through Hartford and the girls stood up in the back seat to film it through the sunroof, the wind almost toppling their skinny frames, hoping it was a good omen, but it disappeared once we arrived in New Haven.

"Keep Francisco home!" Johnny would chant at every protest we held in honor of Francisco. This whole thing has confused Johnny. "Francisco" has come to mean the man in the church, and that man is scared and in danger. As adults, we can all remember the moments when we realized our parents were not infallible, that they were mortal, that they were vulnerable people. But for Johnny, it is happening within a narrative that escapes his comprehension. So he disassociates. He has begun talking about a man named "Francisco" who is his father and about a man named "Daddy" who is also his father. When we go out for pizza, he wants us to bring back a slice of pizza for "Francisco." Francisco is someone who can go hungry if food is not brought to him. (Johnny saves snacks from his school lunch to bring to his father.) On our way to the aquarium one morning, we stopped at a Dunkin' Donuts and Johnny asked for a doughnut with pink frosting and sprinkles. When I passed it to him, he packed up the doughnut in a paper bag real tight, rolled it up, and said, "I am saving this for Francisco." My partner and I insisted he eat it, but he refused. His sisters turned very serious and sad, as if they had seen this behavior before.

I lied and said Francisco gets stomachaches from eating sugar. Only then did he eat it and he ate the doughnut happily, hungrily.

Franny slips into some dissociative moments too. Sometimes she'll speak in the present tense about past events that haven't been true for a year and a half. One evening, Francisco was discussing how he used to wake up very early to go to work at the factory where he worked for fifteen years and Franny said, "What do you mean, Daddy? You still wake up at five A.M. every morning to make it to work." Francisco gently reminded her he didn't. She's having sleep problems. She feels exhausted but cannot reconcile sleep, often until four in the morning, her mind running with thoughts of her father.

The girls were over for a sleepover one night when one of them asked if we planned on buying a house of our own someday, because they'd need their own rooms. We were like, sure someday I mean yeah that's not realistic right now but like sure. We became their emergency contacts at school. I did their makeup for formals and class pictures. They asked my partner to pick them up from places sometimes, no questions asked, and she did. We had our own little Christmas, the four of us, with their first-ever stockings filled with practical presents they were sweet to be excited about, because it wasn't the new Jordans they wanted. When we went to the movies, the four of us would cram into the photo booth, the girls' bony butts sitting on us, and Franny cut out a frame and put it in the back of her phone case. In the winter, we ice-skated in Boston Commons at nightfall as it snowed and in the dead heat of summer we took them to Red Lobster, where I threw up in the parking lot after dinner as they comforted me. Once, the girls asked me why I don't have a New York accent. "Do you know what internalized racism is?" I asked them. They didn't. I told them. I felt loved. I loved them back. We weren't parents but we were something.

I don't want kids of my own. I do not want to be a mother. I have always known this. I have never played with baby dolls. I have never wanted to hold a newborn. I don't want to have to sacrifice anything for a child, I already have too many people to take care of, and I don't want my child to have hazy memories of me in a silk robe with a whiskey ginger ale at 11:00 A.M. acting queerly around bath time, around water—was I . . . trying to drown them? Oh, honey. But my relationship to these kids was different. When we showed up for school functions, I was either assumed to be their young mother or introduced as their mom, by them, with Brianna and Franny grinning wickedly, and I felt like a double agent. But there I was, counting dollar bills to buy Franny's school's bumper sticker to put on our car next to a sticker of soccer-gay-sex-icon Tobin Heath, wasn't I? Where's the lie?!

When I meet kids who suffer, I want to teach them everything I know about the world, which isn't a lot, and basically amounts to: Go to Harvard. Make hella money. Read contracts before you sign them. Bring two tiny bottles of Kahlúa and a tiny bottle of mouthwash when you have to go with your parents to their biopsy results. I follow my own advice while trying to hold off on the suicidal ideation while trying to be as socially fucking mobile as socially fucking possible and then these kids fucking find me, and what do I do, but invite them into my heart and tell them, babes, go to school, climb the ranks, kill the salutatorian, make it look like an accident, and in your valedictory address, remind your school that cops are pigs, and ICE are Nazis, and you are John at the foot of the cross, Jesus's most loved apostle, maybe his lover, and you're in the holy word, escape to my home for some chamomile tea and RuPaul, there will always be room for you, I love you and forever will.

CHAPTER 6

New Haven

It was about an hour before midnight in New York in August and the heat had calmed down just enough to try sleeping. We didn't have working air-conditioning units and our third-floor apartment, built on top of a former garment factory, had a roof with short walls adjacent to our windows, so—this was before the gentrifier snitches got us in trouble with the land-lord—we would drag out our twin-size mattresses through the windows and lay them down on the floor of our roof. The night was still hot but there was a breeze. My mom and dad squeezed onto one mattress and my little brother and I onto the other and I wish I could say we looked up at the stars but there were no stars, per New York's famous light pollution, but there was the moon, and there were the *pop pop pop*s in the background that were either the sound of kids playing with fireworks or the sound of a cop shooting one of us in the back, the odd ice-cream truck playing "Turkey in the Straw" or "Do Your Ears Hang

Low?" which none of us immigrant kids had ever heard before, a car blasting salsa, a woman screaming in drunken ecstasy or else in alarm. The night seemed eternal. My parents were still in their thirties and they were still in love, and I had just watched Beyoncé perform "Crazy in Love" for the first time on TV and I felt electrified. I made my parents promise me they'd never get old. They did, they promised.

My father is in the middle of a prostate cancer scare right now. There is not much to say about it other than he does not want to get a biopsy, against the doctors' advice. The reason he does not want to get the biopsy is because he wants to die. It's two more weeks until we go in to get the results of his next prostate exam and the doctors will probably once again recommend a biopsy and my father will definitely refuse and that will be the moment I have been preparing for my entire life. Everything that I have done or that has happened to me since I took that New York–bound flight twenty-four years ago has been preparing me for this moment—learning English, getting bangs, placing second in the Emancipation Proclamation oratory contest, gaining weight, losing weight, getting the sick puppy from the pet shop, all of that happened to prepare me to this point—my parents are sick, uninsured, and aging out of work in a fucking racist country.

The twisted inversion that many children of immigrants know is that, at some point, your parents become your children, and your own personal American dream becomes making sure they age and die with dignity in a country that has never wanted them. That's what makes caring for our elderly different from Americans caring for their elderly. For one thing, most available jobs for undocumented immigrants are jobs Americans will not do, which takes healthy young migrants and makes them age terribly. At a certain point, manual labor is no longer possible. Aging undocumented people have no safety net. Even though half of undocumented people pay into Social Security, none are eligible for the benefits. They are unable to purchase health insurance. They probably don't own their own homes. They don't have 401(k)s or retirement plans of any kind. Meager savings, if any. Elderly people in general are susceptible to unscrupulous individuals taking advantage of them, and the undocumented community draws even more vultures. According to the Migration Policy Institute, around 10 percent of undocumented people are over fifty-five years old. This country takes their youth, their dreams, their labor, and spits them out with nothing to show for it.

My father is a salad maker now, feeding Manhattan's executive class. I've never watched him make a salad but I'm sure he's exquisite at it. (He did teach me about how to chop a salad in the most efficient way possible, which is to stand as if on a surfboard and take turns balancing your weight on either foot. The rhythm leads to faster chopping.) He has always been the best at his job, no matter the job. He worked as a taxi driver for his first twelve years in America, a time before MapQuest, let alone Uber, and he has the entire city memorized, every axis on the grid, all five boroughs and parts of Jersey. Since then, he has worked in restaurants. Now he is usually the oldest person in the kitchen. Out of respect, the younger guys all call him Don.

Recently, he started a new job, recommended to him by an acquaintance who lured him with the assurance of better hours, better treatment, a better environment. My dad is very gullible.

He spent three days at this new restaurant where, for spare change, they had him work all day, and then in the final hour of the day, he was given just that hour to clean an industrial kitchen, an industrial fryer, a refrigerator, a stove, an oven, and a sink, wash the dishes and the dishwasher, take out the trash, sweep and mop the floors, and clean the garbage chute. His body was wrecked at the end of each day. "I'm too old for this," he said. So he quit. His old job wouldn't take him back. Desperate, he began each morning by showing up at a Latinx job agency, which would send him out to "audition" at a different restaurant day after day, week after week, to no avail.

My dad told me all of this over dinner one night at a hotel restaurant in Midtown Manhattan where I'd invited him to meet me after what I thought was the end of his shift, and it was, but it was the end of a trial shift at a different restaurant than the one I had in mind. This whole thing, all of it, the entire fucking thing, had been kept from me for over a month, per my father's orders, because in my family it is believed I am sometimes *fragile*, stemming back from an incident when I was twenty-one and my father had to come to New Haven in the middle of the night to pick me up from the cold tile of my apartment's bathroom floor, beer bottles and a razor around me, and take me back home to New York. My father had initially refused to enter the restaurant because he believed he wasn't dressed nicely enough for it, but I convinced him my money was good there, and I introduced him to the server as my father in a bit of a *flamboyant* way, not enough to embarrass my dad, just to make a point that this was a motherfucking thing for me and I expected this to be a respected thing among the three of us, and I urged my dad to get the steak and ordered wine for us both and

translated a conversation between the server and my father
about a wine recommendation to go with his meal, which I usually think is so *bourgeois*, and I also joined him when he swirled
the wine in his glass and smelled it, which I also usually think is
the worst, and I quietly slipped myself a Klonopin while he was
cutting his steak, confessing to all of this job trouble, in a pained,
casual way, and then as he kept on talking, boy was there so
much I didn't know, I slipped myself a second Klonopin with
our second glass of wine, and when he left, I went up to my
room and put on the terry-cloth hotel robe and shut off the
lights and passed out feeling nothing, certainly not feeling fragile. I felt like Indio Juan Diego seeing the Virgin of Guadalupe
in her glory, the miracle he wanted and needed at once. I felt
god had gifted me blackness and death and I said, *Thank you
Jehovah God. Thank you. Is this a blackout? I'm free of their tears. Is
this freedom?*

Once his secret was in the open, my dad started texting me
blurry cell phone pictures from the job agency. I told myself I
needed a reminder of why I needed to be successful, so successful, statistical anomaly successful, so I have them saved on my
phone to emotionally blackmail myself with. He took the photos
when he was sitting in the waiting room of the job agency waiting for his name to be called. The first picture is of a man maybe
in his late seventies, wearing a green button-down, khaki pants,
and aviator sunglasses. His lips are downcast. My dad said he
was applying to be a dishwasher. The second picture is of a man
maybe in his late forties who is wearing a black baseball cap, a
gray sweater, and maroon pants. My dad said he'd had a stroke—
his right arm was paralyzed and he had a limp in his right leg.
He was also applying to be a dishwasher. Apparently, he was a

fucking fantastic dishwasher, how, I don't know. When he sent
the pictures, my dad also texted me:

Further proof that we're not a burden.

Who says you're a burden?

*It's hard to see men like that not get jobs. We're invisible because
of the circumstances that force us to be here at the agency . . . old
age . . . illness . . . the fucking papers. Do you understand. A million thoughts rush to my head. It's too much to think about.*

"I hope they have children who can take care of them," I respond.

What I mean to say is: I hope they have a child like me. I hope
everyone has a child like me. If I reach every child of immigrants at an early age, I can make sure every child becomes me.
And if they don't, I can be everyone's child.

Octavio Márquez is a sixty-six-year-old Guatemalan day laborer with a faint white stubble. I saw him in a video online
describing being robbed of his wages by an employer. At some
point in the video he says Americans treat their pets better than
they treat immigrants, which I cannot dispute. I email a message of concern to the immigrant worker center advocating for
Octavio, and receive a reply inviting me to meet him at the blue
boxcar in Brooklyn where the worker center is located. I visit
one morning as the workers are making coffee and eggs. Before
I go in, I stop by a Walgreens and pick out a nice card for Octa-

vio. I stuff it with four hundred dollars. I don't know how much money he was robbed of, but it's what my dad earns in a week so I do it.

Let's talk about money for a second. I've established I grew up poor. Let me guide you through the present day. For my family, poverty is like walking in a hurricane. I buy my parents umbrella after umbrella; each provides some relief, then breaks—cheap fixes, all of them. The rain has paused for now. In Spanish we call that pause escampó. The rain has escampado. It will resume. Right now, I have some discretionary income. But it will not last forever. The guilt I feel having made it out—for now, until my own umbrella breaks—is like having been poisoned. I feel constantly disgusting, dirty, hungover, toxic unless I'm hemorrhaging money in this very specific way that I find *cleansing*.

So what happens is, let's say I go out to dinner. If I'm having an anxious day, I will send my parents take-out dinner. If I see a brown person in the kitchen at the restaurant, I will think that every kitchen in America probably has a Mexican in it and it will make me feel proud but sad—RIP Anthony Bourdain, a homie who got it—and then if my server is brown, if they are either in my opinion too young or too old or seem too tired for the job, I will leave a crazy tip—for what I am, which is a freelancer. Now. I do not have the kind of money to be leaving people crazy tips. But I remember every person who ever left my dad a really good tip when we lived off his tips, I remember *every one*, you don't understand, I have been thinking of those nice Puerto Rican executive assistants for the past fifteen *years*, it was always the Latina executive assistants, very rarely the white people in power, and I remember how he felt for the rest of the evening when he came home. It was like having my dad back from the dead. He would dance to no music and he'd make jokes, and he'd come out of his shower looking like a teenager. I know what a good tip feels like for a poor family. Every good tip feels like Simon helping Jesus carry the cross.

When I am introduced to Octavio I hand him the heavy envelope but it's awkward. I don't know him. I don't tell him there's money in there, but why am I, a total fucking stranger, giving him a greeting card? He keeps forgetting it everywhere so I'm finally like, *Octavio, there's money in there!* He does not open the envelope but puts it away and we're both like, *Fuck what now? Are we friends or something?*

We go to lunch. He's small and appears to be made out of paper. We walk a long time to get to the restaurant and we have the same stride. When we arrive, he's disappointed to hear they've changed management and he doesn't know the owner anymore. He was trying to impress me. He orders stewed ribs and chamomile tea. Octavio tells me that much of the discrimination older immigrants experience is at the hand of younger immigrants. That they will stand within earshot of the older guys and loudly wonder what they're still doing here, or outright say they're too old for the work. But Octavio knows his worth. When an employer picks him to do a job, they always call him back. He says he is friends with a seventy-two-year-old man who makes decorative wooden floors better than anyone else in the game and younger guys can't match his skill.

I ask how he feels on a daily basis as an older man without family here and Octavio says that he feels depressed and anxious. "What kills us is loneliness. I feel lonely even in a room full of people. I feel destabilizing anxiety and pain. Doctors say I don't have anything, but I know I'm sick." I ask Octavio whether his friends have similar problems, and he says they do but their symptoms manifest in different ways. "I think some men who grow old in this country get lost here. They are unfaithful to their wives or turn to alcohol or drugs as a way to blow off steam, to forget their pain. I'd say that out of every hundred older immigrants, ten succumb to depression, anxiety, or worse."

I think about the work of Roberto Gonzales, a Harvard scholar who has conducted longitudinal studies on the effects of undocumented life on young people. As a result of all the stressors of migrant life, he found his subjects suffered chronic headaches, toothaches, ulcers, sleep problems, and eating issues. Which is funny to find in research because I'm twenty-nine and I have this ulcer my doctors can't seem to soothe or diagnose the cause of. It feels like I have an open wound right beneath my breasts in the center of my abdomen and I can feel it spasm and bleed and it never goes away. Sometimes I have to go to Urgent Care, and I drink concoctions and take pills and drink teas and I just keep bleeding, and it hurts the most when, after a long day of reading about people forming human chains to block ICE officers from arresting a man and his child, I sit down to write about my parents.

Now, imagine that thirty, forty, fifty years in. Of course Octavio is sick. We're all fucking *sick*. It is a public health crisis and it's hard to know how to talk about it without feeding into the right-wing propaganda machine that already paints immigrants as charges to the healthcare system and carriers of disease. The trick to doing it is asking Americans to pity us while reassuring them with a myth as old as the country's justifications for slavery—that is, reassuring Americans with the myth that people of color are long-suffering marvels, built to do harder work, built to last longer and handle more, reminding them what America already believes in its soul, which is that we are "impervious to pain," as scholar Robin Bernstein has put it. We can only tell them we're sick if we remind them that sick or not, we are able to still be high-functioning machines.

"I don't feel at home in this country," Octavio says. "Even immigrants in extreme poverty find a way to send their deceased loved ones back home to be buried. They won't be alive to feel happiness again, but they will feel at peace, finally a place to rest. All the dead want is a place to rest." He says this may be his last year before going back to Guatemala. He came here to make enough money to send his kids to school back home, and he did it. One is a mechanic, another is studying law, and the third is an aesthetician—Octavio financed her salon. "Everyone who kills themselves through their work is doing this for their children," he says. "If you don't have kids, why would you kill yourself like this?" For my family the question is, once your kids are grown and doing okay, what happens when you keep killing yourself like this?

I meet Mercedes Soto through Pedro Ituralde, the head of Nuestra Calle, the Staten Island day laborer center, who describes her to me as the best housekeeper he has ever known, which is pretty high fucking praise. She is fifty-six years old but looks a lot older. She has long black hair shot with gray and a round, kind face. I tell her I'm writing about older immigrants and she gasps dramatically, envisioning a world in which she grows old in the United States and takes to living under a bridge. She walks me through the scenario she has envisioned while cracking herself up. "People are going to see me and gossip," she says. "I can't let them do that. They will whisper among themselves, *Have you seen Mercedes? She lives under the bridge now, in a box. She's fallen so far from her days of glory! A ghost of who she used to be!* And then they will avoid saying hi to me because I live under the bridge now. No, ma'am, I'm not going to give them that satisfaction."

She tells me that I remind her of her granddaughter, small and fragile. So when she invites me to her home on Staten Island one afternoon to teach me how to cook small corn cakes called arepas, I immediately say yes. I've never had a grandmother and she seems fun.

Mercedes and her husband rent a small room in a house that she shares with four young Ecuadorian men on the second floor and a young Salvadoran man across the hall from them on the first floor. Mercedes and her husband are, by decades, the oldest people in the house. She is the only woman. The house is spotless, and her room is neatly packed to the brim with belongings. Today, Mercedes is wearing dark-blue Gloria Vanderbilt jeans and a mock-turtleneck sweater, and her hair is in a long braid down her back. She invited her best friend, Monica, to cook with us. She is also fifty-six. ("And she has papers," Mercedes says immediately.) They met at an English class and have been close ever since. Monica has henna-dyed black hair and black eyeliner tattooed on her lids. She suggests I am wearing too much makeup.

The women do not let me cook. Latina women never let me cook. I used to have this self-mythology about my upbringing, which is that my parents never taught me to cook because they didn't want to teach me skills that would make me a good housewife—my mother's biggest fear—since whenever I asked to help them in the kitchen, they sent me to go read a book. So I was like, I had feminist parents! But now I realize that the literal truths about myself that are immediately manifest to others—I am clumsy, distracted, have no attention to detail, am messy, fall often, hurt myself easily—made me clearly useless in the kitchen and they just didn't want me around to interfere. When I have tried cooking for various older Latinas, they always take over immediately, not because they're feminist vigilantes, but because they're perfectionists and they are good at what they do and why would they let me make a mess of things? To *indulge* me?

Monica assembles a growing pile of arepas next to her. To make them, you mix white corn flour, warm water, butter, salt, and cheese in a bowl. You set it aside to cool, then take out the sticky dough and knead it. Monica uses a drinking glass to press perfect circles into the dough. Mercedes has made Mexican champorrado, a thick hot chocolate with oatmeal and molasses. It is already simmering when I arrive.

Mercedes and her husband, Jacinto, plan on "retiring" in a couple of years. That means they'll stop working in the United States and move back to Mexico, probably to work in some much more relaxed capacity there. He is a gardener and, at sixty-two years old, finds himself going head-to-head with younger men. His lower back kills him and he gets overheated easily. He refused to go to the doctor for a long time—*I'm fine, leave me alone!*—but Mercedes put her foot down, issued an ultimatum, and he went to the community health clinic, which charges twenty dollars for a visit. "I can't love you more than you love yourself," she told him. "Grown children will not take care of you when you're older—especially boys, and we have boys." Monica agrees that being a mother to adult sons with their own families to take care of makes her feel vulnerable. Jacinto comes to the kitchen to eat and drink with us. He is shy and laughs quietly at his wife's jokes but speaks up when we begin to talk about adult children. "I don't want to have to extend my hand to them to ask for food," he says firmly. Plus, the children can be demanding, expecting too much of their parents. One day, Mercedes's son raised his voice at her on the phone because he needed her and didn't know where she was. "The day I live in your house and you spoon-feed me, I'll listen to you, but until then, I'll do as my heart desires," she told him.

The following night, I take a taxi to a church on Staten Island where Nuestra Calle is having a Christmas party. Mercedes is being honored for helping out in the community. The tables are covered in red plastic cloths and sprinkled with snowflake glitter confetti. I sit with Monica and Jacinto. Their phones ping with automated Bible-scripture text messages in a huge font that they have to hold far from their faces in order to read. We eat plates of baked ziti as we watch teenagers in plush antlers dance with each other. There is a live band, a group of men in pink blazers with accordions. There's a toddler in a tiny matching blazer and tiny matching accordion pretending to play along. Mercedes and Jacinto show me a picture of their religious marriage ceremony, which took place recently, forty-two years after their civil one. She looks like a teen bride, wearing a white princess dress and a tiara. I walk from table to table, complimenting all the women's makeup and asking if anyone wants to talk about aging, which you know, I'm no Ronan Far-row. One woman stops me to say she wants her story told. Al-tagracia is nearly fifty years old and is recovering from surgery to remove a cyst in her uterus that she had unsuccessfully tried to self-treat with herbs from a naturalist. She wants to tell me that she was conned by a woman in Mexico who said she could expedite her green-card petition and soon began extorting her for ever-increasing fees with the threat of being turned in to ICE if she did not comply. Altagracia paid her a total of twelve thousand dollars.

Because of her poor health, Altagracia has death on her mind and is thinking about going back to Mexico. "There was a raid on a 7-Eleven near my house just last week. And the other day on the bus, a white woman went on a racist rant against me while I was just standing there. All of the racism here makes me want to go back to my country when I die. I'm not wanted here, and I do not want to live in eternity in a place where I'm not wanted." In the meantime, she says, her plan for aging involves her two children. She tells me a story about a woman she some-times sees when she goes out to collect recycling for cash. The woman is seventy years old and collects recycling for a living. She was widowed when she was very young and never remar-ried, never had children. Now, Altagracia says, the woman is all alone and left to die in a foreign country without anyone to take care of her. She says the lesson is that it is important to have children who can take care of us when we grow old.

"You can't guarantee how your kids are going to turn out. There are good children and there are bad children, so in my opinion, people should have two kids. One of them ought to turn out well. I have two kids, and after my surgery, there was always one of them around to take care of me when the other

one was busy." An heir and a spare. I ask her if the pressure of
that might be hard on the children.

"Perhaps," she says. "But that's the tradition."

Early the next morning, I visit Nuestra Calle. There are just
five older men sitting inside, out of the cold. One of the men
recognizes me from the party and says with a large grin, "I remember you. You tried to interview me, but I didn't want to
talk to you." I concede that that was me, and try again. He leans
back in his chair and sucks his teeth, thinking awhile. "No," he
concludes. I sit down to drink my coffee and we make small
talk, until we're kicked out by a woman who wants to sweep the
space.

Outside, I lean against the façade. The men gather around me
in a semicircle. The man to my right, in his sixties, wearing a
red New York Yankees baseball cap and a brown hoodie, too
light for the cold, starts talking bitterly about the life of a migrant. He says he has completely given up, and that's what he
says, but here he is, isn't he, at 7:00 A.M. on a freezing morning,
clocking in like the rest of us. The other men quickly interrupt
him, tenderly, in hushed tones. They urge him to get help. I shut
up and listen. A picture begins to form. He is homeless and ad-
dicted to alcohol. The men try to tell him that he has to stare
down a childhood trauma in order to get better, rather than
escaping from his pain with drink. They tell him he is the smart-
est man they know, the most eloquent, and they don't want to
see this end badly. It's an intervention.

It seems spur of the moment, brought on by the opportunity
to speak about the suffering of migration in the third person,

almost pedagogically. He gets mad at them, but they're very loving toward him. When he walks away, they tell me they are the lucky ones, that old day laborers often end up sick, sad, and alone, too embarrassed and lonely to go to the worker centers, instead picking up work in remote corners. "But I wouldn't advise you to go to those places alone," the man who turned down the interview says. "If you want to go there, we'll go with you."

I am ten years older than my brother. I have always imagined us as being part of an "heir and spare" sort of situation, which I know about because my mother is obsessed with the European royal families—she thinks I look like Charlotte Casiraghi of Monaco the way my father thinks I have the spirit of Greta Thunberg. I . . . don't. My brother has always been so *level-headed*, so *sweet*, and *patient*, and—I say this with absolute awe and relief—has never shown signs of mental illness, so my parents were grateful for him, grateful that he was healthy and fine, grateful that he was spared. He's not crazy, sure. But he was also born in Brooklyn. Which means he's an American citizen.

Whereas it was my responsibility to be the face of the family, the hunter, the gatherer, my brother just had to find it in him to do his homework. He was Prince Harry. He just had to . . . not be photographed in a Nazi costume. But he also had a bigger responsibility than I had, that I could not have because I was my parents' undocumented child. He just had to turn twenty-one.

Every mixed-status family in the United States knows the drill. An undocumented parent can be sponsored by their American-citizen child when the child turns twenty-one. (This does not work for siblings or other family members.) My parents never talked about it around my brother, though surely it made them hopeful, but I thought about it all the time. I took to lovingly calling him my little anchor baby, after the disparaging term Republicans used for the American-born children of undocumented immigrants who supposedly "anchored" them to the United States. I reclaimed the term. On his birthday, I always took him out to dinner, and as he ate his sushi happily and cluelessly, I'd think, *You beautiful aging casket of wine. Better by the day.*

This all changed recently, when reports began circulating that ICE was arresting undocumented parents and spouses of American citizens when they petitioned for green cards. Immigration lawyers began advising children, husbands, and wives against petitioning for them at all.

Ricardo Reyes, a twenty-one-year-old recent Yale graduate, is one of those kids. He is an American citizen. He has the face and demeanor of an adorable bludgeoned baby seal. His parents worked in the garment industry in Los Angeles for decades before moving to the Pacific Northwest to make a living picking apples. "Since I was in elementary school, I would hear my mom talk about naturalization," he told me. He was their oldest child, so he'd reach the finish line first. He and several of his friends at Yale, also the children of immigrants, were turning twenty-one within a few months of each other and they were counting down the days, talking excitedly after class about who would turn twenty-one first. Then on the morning of his birthday, his lawyer told him it would be too risky to file an application. One of his classmates had seen her dad detained during their green card interview, and he was deported despite a national outcry.

After digesting the news, Ricardo's mother announced that

when her body can no longer withstand picking apples she'd like to go back to Mexico. His father has been here since he was nineteen years old, so it's hard for him to imagine returning to Mexico, but Ricardo thinks he'll probably end up going back too. Ricardo is devastated that he wasn't able to adjust their legal status but finds comfort in the fact that he can provide for their retirement if they go back to Mexico. He is a middle school teacher now, back in L.A. "Any money I make will not be for me. I just need an apartment. The rest will be for my parents." I take him out to drinks and am like, how about chemical engineering, baby? But he wants to be a teacher and I admire that purity even if I have no high hopes for its financial output.

But Ricardo is young, and for now his parents can still work. He does not yet know what this life will do to him. I'm looking to interview children of immigrants partly to get a blueprint for myself because I'm lost and I am scared, so I set off to find somebody a little older, someone who has been doing this for a while, and in my research I stumble upon thirty-six-year-old Mira Fernández. Mira is a Latina journalist who writes for the local Spanish paper who counts my dad as one of her readers. She grew up in New York, the daughter of undocumented immigrants. Her dad was a day laborer, and she lived with her parents—and paycheck to paycheck—until she was an adult. She remembers that, one month, after paying her bills and rent, she had no money left over to buy sanitary napkins, so she bought a roll of toilet paper that she made last her whole period. It was humiliating. "I decided that would never happen again. I wanted to save up so I could retire one day, and I was going to provide for my parents' emotional health and quality of life," she tells me. She did not want to be able to provide only for their

basic needs. She wanted them to live with dignity. So she began
to work toward that.

Then, after decades as a day laborer, her father started to
show signs of depression. His years had consisted of going
to work, coming home to sleep, going to work, coming home to
sleep, and back again, with nothing in his life to give it meaning
or pleasure. He got older. He became overcome by stress and
anxiety. He stopped talking. This is when Mira started noticing
the miniature cars. They were the size of Hot Wheels cars, but
they were built with intricate detail, like built-to-scale models.
Her dad soon began amassing dozens, tens of dozens of tiny
cars. He was skilled in woodwork, so after work or on weekends,
during any free time he had, he would work on an elaborate
wooden display for the cars. He'd clean them lovingly with
small cotton rounds. He painted any scratches they had, and he
rearranged them constantly. It's the only way he passed the
time when he was home. I ask Mira if this made her sad. She is
quiet for a long time, then says, "You know, he filled up this
space in his heart with those little cars, so I'm just glad he found
a way to feel better."

After many years of trying, Mira's parents, now much older,
could not do manual labor in the United States anymore and
went back to Mexico. Mira fully supports them, sending money
twice a month. I ask her what percentage of her paycheck goes
to her parents, and she says it is something she does so naturally
and so much, she's never even thought to calculate that.

"Look, they're better off there," she says. "They were tired of
their lives here. Their emotional health is more stable there,
they have their own home, they have activities, they have friends.
Here, they worked constantly just to make ends meet, just to

pay rent on time. They could not retire here, but with some financial help on my part, their lives over there are more peaceful." She admits it is financially complicated for her, but her parents always express their gratitude and they never ask for money outright. "I'd feel guilty not doing it, but I'm very happy to be able to do it, and I'm very happy to help them," she says.

Her brother doesn't contribute. He says he has his own family to take care of. Mira theorizes that Latin American culture is so imbued with patriarchal values that paint women as natural caregivers and nurturers that women feel a greater responsibility toward aging parents, and women who are not able to balance or reject those values feel an inescapable burden.

I used to say that I would slip antifreeze into my brother's coffee (it has a sweet taste, and he likes how I prepare his coffee, dulce and light enough that it should match my skin tone) if he did not help me take care of our parents as they aged. Once, he was maybe twelve years old and his report card was pretty bad. His report cards were pretty bad from his first ever one in kindergarten until he was in community college, so this was not a surprise—we all have our strengths and academics was not his. But it was a fucking nightmare for a family so focused on social mobility—and I was *pissed*. I called him on the phone and screamed at the top of my lungs that as an American citizen, he was wasting his opportunities, and that if he ended up working at a Best Buy and not going to college, I would never speak to him again in my life. "You hear that? I have no problem cutting you off. Don't you try me. You won't be a burden to me. I will never fucking talk to you *again*." I recently apologized to him for being so cruel and he just laughed and said he didn't take me seriously because I was just like Dad.

When my father could drive—before he started dying—he would take me to the Land of Make Believe or Splish Splash or some other tristate-area water park every summer. He did it because commercials for water parks were featured prominently on local television and they depicted children acting carefree and wild and I was not carefree or wild and it weighed on him, so he insisted I try. I did not know how to swim. He tried to teach me but I was terrified of the water. My father is prone to anger and so he is not a good teacher. When he made me practice long division at home and I got answers wrong, he'd rip up the pages I worked on about an inch from my face while telling me I was stupid. He took that approach to swimming lessons, and after a few minutes, he'd usually just storm off and my mother would tell me to ignore him. Through adulthood, my friends treated my not knowing how to swim like my not knowing how to ride a bicycle or not being able to leave the country— just, like, a quirky thing about me.

My fear of water and inability to swim did not stop my father from taking me to water parks. It made him more dogged in pursuit of the activity. It's all he wanted to do in the summers. My mother packed sandwiches and snacks because concession food was too expensive, and off we went. The only ride I could tolerate was the Lazy River because all I had to do was float on an inner tube, but my father liked for us to go on the rides with long, dark tubes that twisted into crazy loops at high speed and then spat you out into a pool. Those rides had long lines, and the entire way up I would have a pit in my stomach and I pleaded with him not to make me go. He insisted it would be fun, the whole point was my having fun. He'd go first, then wait at the bottom. At the top of the ride, when I was standing barefoot on a warm wooden landing and there was a dark tunnel in front of me filled with a fast current of water rushing into the pitch black, the people who worked at the ride would *repeatedly* ask me if I was okay going down. But I didn't want to face my father if I gave up, so I lay down in the tube, crossed my arms, counted to three, and pushed myself down. Years later, my psychiatrist would tell me that my anxiety and adrenaline run on the same "train tracks," so I often get them confused. If I experienced an adrenaline rush in the dark tubes, or if I experienced a panic attack while I was in them, I cannot say. I remember it as a sharp intake of breath, down to the cold of my soul. And I remember the next moment of awareness, which is being spit into a pool, and sinking.

I sank. I always sank. I knew I could stand, but my body was leaden and I fell at the wrong angle. And my father always reached down and brought me to air, my long black hair stuck to my face. I was never underwater long enough to come up gasping for air, but I can still feel the taste of chlorine in my lungs. I miss the taste of chlorinated pool water. And I miss this dynamic, of my father putting me in a manufactured scene of crisis in which I would feel helpless but at the same time be perfectly safe. I felt like I was going to die, but I would not die. A person who cannot swim and who panics in water is in danger in a pool, and my father knew that, and he made it so that he could save me every time. It was never a big production when he did it, he'd just pick me up by the armpits and say, "Wasn't that *fun?*" I think the lesson was: He was my father, and he was god. As long as I would panic and sink, and he could save me, he would always have that place.

I never learned to swim. The farthest I had ever ventured into the ocean was to my knees, screaming the whole while. But by last summer, right before I turned twenty-nine and he turned fifty-four, our roles had so profoundly reversed and his self-esteem was so devastatingly low that I wondered if I could give that back to him, this ability to save me. Like the water-park drownings, this invitation was also perfectly manufactured: I invited him to come spend an afternoon at the beach in the middle of July precisely with the purpose of teaching me how to swim. It would take, max, three hours and I would take, just, one Klonopin.

The beach we went to is called Lighthouse Point. It's on the Long Island Sound, not far from New Haven. The Long Island Sound is technically an estuary, which is where salt water from the ocean and fresh water from rivers mix. Sixteen different very New Englandy rivers empty out into the Atlantic Ocean at this spot. Emma Lazarus wrote a forgettable poem about it with not a huddling mass in sight. It is described in *The Great Gatsby* as "the most domesticated body of salt water in the Western hemisphere." When I was in college, I got the coordinates of East Egg and West Egg, fictional places on Long Island, tattooed by my left breast because they symbolized my desire for what I cannot have. But now, I just like this beach because there are always black and brown families fishing or building sand castles there, proudly being alive, and there is just something about the ocean air perfuming dark bodies refusing to die that makes me want to live another day too.

To begin, my father poured cold water over my body with his hands like a priest baptizing an infant. It was freezing. His arms were very white. My father had not been to the beach in seven years. He told me the first step was being able to stand in deep water, which he likened to standing on a packed subway when you don't have a pole to hold and cannot lean against a door. Your legs have to be apart just so, and you use your arms to stabilize yourself. He asked me to shift my weight from foot to foot as if I was on a bumpy subway ride, I guess kind of like he stands when he chops lettuce. He grabbed my hand and we went deeper into the ocean until the water was up to my chest, the deepest I had ever gone. "Next, you float," he told me. He grabbed my hands and asked me to go on my stomach, extend my legs as far as they would go, and kick. He assured me he would not let go. I told him I weighed 140 pounds, which is not true, laadeedaa, but he said it didn't matter, and to prove that to me, he asked me to grab him by the hands and he told me I would be able to support his entire weight in the water. "The water will help you carry my weight," he said.

I did. I mean the water did. When it was my turn, I asked him to swear to not let me go. I'd usually ask him to swear on his mother, because I know that's what he holds most holy, but I think she's demonic so I don't like bringing her up. Instead, I asked why I should believe him. As an adult, he has told me that because he is a good father, he has lied to me my whole life, and he is proud of lying to me, and he will lie to me until he dies, so his word means nothing from him. I held on to his hands so tightly I am sure I bruised them. He did not let go.

But I did not float. My body is not buoyant. "Your body is determined to sink," my father announced as he tried to hold me up by the stomach. My legs do not extend in the water, so I cannot kick; they gravitate toward my father's body like a magnet and I sink. I sink, but not down. My legs sink laterally, toward his body, so I end up vertical. He relaxed his body and showed me how easy it was to float on his back—Mire!—totally flat, but in my resting state, my body in water wants to be upright, on my feet. Both of us realized at the same time that this was a true thing about me, and we tried to change it until finally our limbs gave out and we returned to shore. I was not able to restore the natural order of things.

Back on sand, I asked him if, before, on the roof that summer, he had lied when he promised to stay young forever.

Yes, he said.

If you break little promises you'll break big ones. That's what you said.

I know. But I won't.

My mom was on a beach blanket, her back to the sun, trying to darken the skin around a scar. She didn't turn around to look at my dad and he didn't look at her. Now that I think of it, they didn't speak to each other at all that day except for when they awkwardly waded into the water together and stood some space apart, looking like two dead fish in the ocean together, stagnant but afloat. And that's how they planned to stay, dead, stagnant, and afloat, even after we discovered that my dad wasn't going to watch volleyball on weekends after all, even after I confronted him and he admitted it but blamed my mom. I separated them. He left home one night while my mom and brother were at church and I reminded him to write my brother a loving text because that night would be hard for him.

There is research about migrant families, but children do not see it as prophecies foretold. I should have known better. I had spoken to a lot of people telling me the same things. And now here it was happening to my family, my soccer team, the world's best. Shortly before I asked him to leave, my father had told my brother: "I am tired of living just for you and your sister. It is my turn to be happy now." And he handled it the wrong way, totaled some people's lives in his wake, but he was right. It was his turn to be happy. And now my mom is free to figure out what makes her happy, after thirty-one years. Thirty of those years have been spent here in America, being undocumented together. She goes to yoga now. The other day, she had a *hot dog*.

I asked almost everyone I interviewed for this book about regrets, but they didn't tell me many. That's not what they remember of their time here. That's not what we'll remember when we have to leave, by choice, force, or casket. The look in a mother's eyes at her baby's first word in English, my father's heaving sobs when I handed him my diploma in Latin from the best fucking school in the world, Leonel's first steps of freedom outside the church in the autumn cold after four months in hiding, the Mexican chefs behind every great restaurant in New York, the Upper East Side babies who love their Haitian nannies so much it makes their moms jealous, a day laborer's first cold shower in America after wearing off the soles of his feet in the desert, the two young men who pushed Joaquín up the mountain when he wanted to die, Jesus Christ himself on the cross—*Truly I tell you, whatever you did for one of the least of these brothers and sisters of mine, you did for me.*

ACKNOWLEDGMENTS

—— ◇ ——

This book would not have been possible without Cindy Spiegel and Julie Grau. All thanks go to Emi Ikkanda for her patience, wisdom, and bravery, for championing this odd little book and my odd little voice. To my agent Peter Steinberg for making it all happen and for always believing in a freak like me. To Cecil Flores, you're the best. Most of all, thanks to Christopher Jackson, who taught me how to write out of clarity and not anger, and whom I'd trust to lobotomize my brain to match his, no anesthesia.

My editors and mentors throughout the years who have watched over me since I was a teenager—thanks go to Theodore Ross, Sasha Frere-Jones, Ben Metcalf, Jim Dao, Ryu Spaeth, Rachel Ronsenfelt, Dayna Tortorici, Nikil Saval, and Kara Vanderbijil for my first breaks.

There were moments in my life when I needed critical support and Susan and Chip Fisher, Jason Wright, the Ellsworth and

Sanger families, and Jessica Switzer Pliska were selfless and nurturing. I can never return the kindness.

To Laurene Powell Jobs, for support of my work and my vision. To Amy Low, Peter Lattman, and Alex Simon.

To Meg White.

At Yale, I owe everything to Allegra di Bonaventura. To my closest advisor and mentor, Kathryn Dudley, for teaching me how to write with empathy for the living, the dead, and the never alive; to Albert Laguna for reserving compliments until I deserved them; to Laura Wexler for encouraging me to think wild and big; to Sally Promey for her unwavering belief in me; to Mary Liu for never giving up on me even when I had, and to Glenda Carpio, Alicia Schmidt Camacho, and Steve Pitti for paving the way.

Thank you to Brad Weston, Pam Abdy, Scott Nemes, Jonás Cuaron, and Richie Kern.

To Sam Baum, for believing in a girl from the wrong side of the tracks.

To the activists from whom I've learned so much, thank you for welcoming me into your world—Gonzalo Mercado, Aurora Saucedo, John Jairo Lugo, Vanesa Suarez, Charla Nich, and Gini King.

To Dan Berger and Jonah Vorspan-Stein.

To my friends Stephanie Rodriguez, Christopher Kramaric, Pierre Berastaín, Shelby Kinney-Lang, Annie Badman, Mira Lippold-Johnson, Carolee Klimchock, Carole Anderson, Moira Donegan, Nico Olarte-Hayes, Adam Berkwitt, and Jordi Oliveres.

To my neighbors Anne, Dave, Tal, Tovah, and to Bitsie, Luna, Oscar, Nickel, Annie, Mako, Sal, Phife, and Bobcat. Thank you for taking care of me.

To Dr. Brian Frankel.

To the Alroys, Zemachs, Bersins, Lawlers, Stovalls, Fischstroms, to Twyla Silva and Anne Rosenthal. Special thanks to Kaethe, David, and Bucca.

To my uncle Darwin—you're an inspiration to me. My eyes are on what you and your boys will accomplish in the years to come. I strive every day to be a little bit more like you. You're my hero. Kenneth and Jullian—work hard.

To my squirrels.

To my little brother, Derek—thank you for holding down the fort, for being patient and wise and for being our rock. You are the chosen one. It's your job now to carry on the torch. You are Frodo and I am Gollum.

To TZB and Frankie Rodham, my chosen family, the ones who taught me that love could be joyful and it didn't have to hurt. You are my safe space. Thank you for healing me.

To my mother, who should have had a different life, I will do everything in my power to give you a different future. I am the woman I am today because of you. And I am proud of the strong, ferocious woman you keep becoming every day.

Finally, to my father—you'll never know what it is like to carry your father's heart in yours when it has been so torn to shreds for your sake. I will circle the world many times over telling everyone about its weight, its beauty, and what an honor it was to have known it.

NOTES

CHAPTER 1: Staten Island

7 **By way of comparison, Brooklyn and Queens:** Ben Adler, "Brooklyn's Median Household Income Is Less Than $45,000," *Slate*, January 9, 2014, http://www.slate.com/articles/business/moneybox/2014/01/new_york_city_census_data_manhattan_and_brooklyn_are_much_poorer_than_you.html; United States Census Bureau, "Bronx County (Bronx Borough), New York, V2017," https://www.census.gov/quickfacts/fact/table/bronxcountybronxboroughnewyork/PST045217; United States Census Bureau, "New York County (Manhattan Borough), New York, V2017," https://www.census.gov/quickfacts/fact/table/newyorkcountymanhattanboroughnewyork/BZA210216; United States Census Bureau, "Queens County (Queens Borough), New York, V2017," https://www.census.gov/quickfacts/fact/table/queenscountyqueensboroughnewyork/PST045216; United States Census Bureau, "Kings County (Brooklyn Borough), New York, V2017," https://www.census.gov/quickfacts/fact/table/kingscountybrooklynboroughnewyork/PST045217.

7 **Governor Mario Cuomo insisted that the referendum be approved:** David Colon, "Brexit Has Staten Island Councilman Calling for Secession, 'Regardless of Cost,'" *Gothamist*, June 27, 2016, http://gothamist.com/2016/06/27/k_bye.php.

7 **Staten Island is the city's most conservative borough:** John O'Connor, "An Outlier in City Politics, Staten Island at the Center of National Politi-

cal Trends," WNYC, December 28, 2017, https://www.wnyc.org/story
/outlier-city-politics-staten-island-center-national-political-trends/.

8 **It's also the borough where Eric Garner:** Ray Sanchez, "Protests After
N.Y. Cop Not Indicted in Chokehold Death; Feds Reviewing Case," CNN
.com, December 4, 2014, http://www.cnn.com/2014/12/03/justice/new
-york-grand-jury-chokehold/index.html.

8 **There was fifty-two-year-old Alejandro Galindo:** Andy Humm, "Behind
the Hate Crimes on Staten Island," *Gotham Gazette*, August 23, 2010,
http://www.gothamgazette.com/civil-rights/583-behind-the-hate-crimes
-on-staten-island.

8 **They beat him with a baseball bat:** Frank Donnelly, "Staten Island Hate
Crime Suspect Indicted on Robbery, Assault Charges After Allegedly
Beating Up Mexican Immigrant," SILive.com, August 6, 2010, updated
January 3, 2019, http://www.silive.com/northshore/index.ssf/2010/08
/suspect_in_staten_island_hate.html.

8 **"We believe at this time that they selected":** Nicole Bliman, "NY Police:
4 Face Hate Crime Charges in Beating of Mexican Man," CNN.com, April
10, 2010, http://www.cnn.com/2010/CRIME/04/10/hate.crime.arrests
/index.html.

9 *The New York Times* **describes their work:** Joseph Berger, "For Day
Laborers, Used to Scraping By, Hurricane Creates a Wealth of Work," *The
New York Times*, December 30, 2012, https://www.nytimes.com/2012/12
/31/nyregion/day-laborers-find-steady-work-after-hurricane-sandy.html.

9 **A 2006 survey of day laborers, who are mostly men, reports that:** Hec-
tor Cordero-Guzman, Elizabeth Pantaleon, and Martha Chavez, "Day
Labor, Worker Centers & Disaster Relief Work in the Aftermath of Hurricane Sandy," School of Public Affairs, Baruch College, October 30, 2013,
p. 3, https://www.dropbox.com/s/vnspe6ir243jpz7/Aftermath%20of%20
Hurricane%20Sandy%20Report-FINAL.11.4.13.pdf?dl=0.

11 **There are now more than sixty-three worker centers:** Ibid., pp. 4–5.

13 **It gave law enforcement officials the power:** The CAP Immigration
Team, "Top 5 Negative Impacts of Arizona's 'Papers Please' Law," *American Progress*, April 20, 2012, https://www.americanprogress.org/issues
/immigration/news/2012/04/20/11425/top-5-negative-impacts-of
-arizonas-papers-please-law/.

24 **Hurricane Sandy hit the night of October 29:** Special Initiative for Re-
building and Resiliency, "Chapter 1: Sandy and Its Impacts," in *A Stronger,
More Resilient New York* (New York: Government of New York City, 2013),
p. 11, http://www.nyc.gov/html/sirr/downloads/pdf/final_report/Ch_1
_SandyImpacts_FINAL_singles.pdf.

25 **During this same period, New Orleans mayor:** Daniel A. Farber and Jim
Chen, *Disasters and the Law: Katrina and Beyond* (New York: Aspen Publish-
ers, 2006), p. 141.

25 **The first and biggest contractor to come on the scene:** Joel Roberts, "Report: Katrina Cleanup Too Expensive," CBS News, May 4, 2006, https://www.cbsnews.com/news/report-katrina-cleanup-too-expensive/; Isadora Rangel, "Republican Attack Ads Blast Randy Perkins' Company," TCPalm.com, October 27, 2016, https://www.tcpalm.com/story/news/politics/elections/2016/10/27/randy-perkins-company-ashbritt/91214744/.

25 **The company left behind two EPA-designated superfund sites:** Jarret Renshaw, "Democratic Lawmakers Say AshBritt Has Poor Environmental Track Record," *The Star-Ledger*, March 7, 2013, updated March 30, 2019, https://www.nj.com/politics/index.ssf/2013/03/democratic_lawmakers_say_ashbr.html.

25 **There were forty drowning deaths:** Laura Petrecca, "Majority of Superstorm Sandy Deaths Were from Drowning," *USA Today*, May 23, 2013, https://www.usatoday.com/story/news/2013/05/23/superstorm-sandy-deaths-red-cross-cdc-drowning/2354559/.

26 **The storm caused $62 billion:** Adam Jeffery, "Five Years On: A Look Back at the Destruction Caused by Superstorm Sandy," CNBC.com, October 30, 2017, https://www.cnbc.com/2017/10/30/five-years-on-a-look-back-at-the-destruction-caused-by-superstorm-sandy.html.

27 **They cleaned flooded basements, removed fallen branches:** https://ndlon.org/after-hurricane-sandy-day-laborers-play-central-role-in-cleanup-rebuilding-2/.

30 **The bell at the church rang at one o'clock:** "Este fin de semana sepultaron a Ubaldo Cruz en Xayacatlán," *Puebla Noticias*, November 12, 2012, http://www.pueblanoticias.com.mx/noticia/este-fin-de-semana-sepultaron-a-ubaldo-cruz-en-xayacatlan-28383/.

CHAPTER 2: Ground Zero

32 **But days went by and only:** Celeste Katz and J. K. Dineen, "Rescued from Debris," *New York Daily News*, September 12, 2001.

32 **it soon became clear that the mapping technology:** Ford Fessenden, "A Nation Challenged: Ground Zero; Fire Dept. Has Pinpointed 700 New Human Remains," *The New York Times*, March 26, 2002.

32 **Thermal heat maps from NASA:** Roger N. Clark et al., *Images of the World Trade Center Site Show Thermal Hot Spots on September 16 and 23, 2001* (Denver: U.S. Department of the Interior, U.S. Geological Survey, 2001).

33 *New Scientist* **dubbed it:** Jonathan Beard, "Ground Zero's Fires Still Burning," *New Scientist*, December 3, 2001, https://www.newscientist.com/article/dn1634-ground-zeros-fires-still-burning/.

33 **The nearly three thousand human beings who died:** Paul J. Lioy, *Dust: The Inside Story of Its Role in the September 11th Aftermath* (Lanham, Md.: Rowman & Littlefield, 2010), pp. 44, 96, 253–54.

35 **the James Zadroga 9/11 Health and Compensation Act:** Rupa Bhattacharyya, *Seventh Annual Status Report and Third Annual Reassessment of Policies and Procedures,* September 11th Victim Compensation Fund, February 2019, https://www.vcf.gov/pdf/VCFStatusReportFeb2019.pdf.

41 **Rafael was declared to have:** Associated Press, "Death of Mexican 9/11 Worker Raises Questions," CBS News, January 16, 2012, https://www.cbsnews.com/news/death-of-mexican-9-11-worker-raises-questions/.

41 **In a Fox News Latino television interview taped:** Elizabeth Llorente, "On Sept. 11, a Mexican Firefighter Followed His Instincts and Ran into the Twin Towers," Fox News, September 27, 2011, updated January 4, 2017, http://www.foxnews.com/politics/2011/09/08/mexican-immigrant-has-no-regrets-about-risking-his-life-to-help-on-sept-11-even.html.

42 **And New York State, as well as most:** Ted Hesson, "Five Ways Immigration System Changed After 9/11," ABC News, September 11, 2012, http://abcnews.go.com/ABC_Univision/News/ways-immigration-system-changed-911/story?id=17231590.

52 **"the gatekeeper to the official list":** Anthony DePalma, *City of Dust: Illness, Arrogance, and 9/11* (Upper Saddle River, N.J.: Pearson FT Press, 2010), pp. 180, 192.

53 **A few weeks after the towers fell:** Amy Waldman, "A Nation Challenged: Mementos; With Solemn Detail, Dust of Ground Zero Is Put in Urns," *The New York Times,* October 15, 2001, https://www.nytimes.com/2001/10/15/nyregion/nation-challenged-mementos-with-solemn-detail-dust-ground-zero-put-urns.html.

53 **The Mexican consulate held its own memorial:** Alexandra Délano, Benjamin Nienass, Anna Lisa Tota, and Trevor Hagen, "Making Absence Present: The September 11 Memorial," in *Routledge International Handbook of Memory Studies,* eds. Anna Lisa Tota and Trevor Hagen (New York: Routledge, 2016), p. 405.

56 **EN MEMORIA DE LOS DELIVERY BOYS:** Michael Raisch, "September 11th Delivery Bike Memorial," Raisch Studios, http://www.raischstudios.com/911-messenger-bike/.

57 **There was Antonio Meléndez, and Antonio Javier Álvarez:** "Mexicanos del 9/11: La tumba del olvido," *Huffington Post,* September 11, 2012, https://www.huffingtonpost.com/2012/09/11/mexicanos-world-trade-center_n_1872849.html.

57 **There was also Fernando Jimenez Molinar:** Wilbert Torre, "Los mexicanos olvidados," *El Mundo,* September 10, 2006, http://archivo.eluniversal.com.mx/internacional/51524.html.

CHAPTER 3: Miami

60 **The city of Hialeah in Miami-Dade County:** "Miss Earhart Flies to Miami," *The New York Times,* May 24, 1937.

63 **I've seen white people carry signs plastered:** Bill Chappell, "A Father and Daughter Who Drowned at the Border Put Attention on Immigration," NPR, June 26, 2019, https://www.npr.org/2019/06/26/736177694 /a-father-and-daughter-drowned-at-the-border-put-attention-on -immigration.

64 **Researchers have shown that the flooding of stress hormones:** William Wan, "What Separation from Parents Does to Children: 'The Effect Is Catastrophic,'" *The Washington Post,* June 18, 2018, https://www.washingtonpost .com/national/health-science/what-separation-from-parents-does-to -children-the-effect-is-catastrophic/2018/06/18/c00c30ec-732c-11e8 -805c-4b67019fcfe4_story.html?fbclid=IwAR2TZtOIZSTk1QX1pgmrSI 9ggEelQfo8dbVtf80fKLH8KICU20ApnD_TMu0&utm_term= .e52cf1a5bcdb.

65 **the House of Representatives voted:** Thomas Kaplan and Robert Pear, "House Passes Measure to Repeal and Replace the Affordable Care Act," *The New York Times,* May 4, 2017, https://www.nytimes.com/2017/05/04 /us/politics/health-care-bill-vote.html; Lily Herman, "Getting Treated for Rape Could Be Considered a Preexisting Condition Under the GOP's Health Care Plan," *Allure,* May 4, 2017, https://www.allure.com/story /sexual-assault-pre-existing-condition-republican-health-care-plan.

65 **Experts estimated it would strip healthcare:** Robert Pear, "G.O.P. Health Bill Would Leave 23 Million More Uninsured in a Decade, C.B.O. Says," *The New York Times,* May 24, 2017, https://www.nytimes.com/2017/05 /24/us/politics/cbo-congressional-budget-office-health-care.html.

65 **Miami-Dade has the state's largest number:** Daniel Chang, "With High Uninsured Rate, Miami-Dade Faces Health Crisis, Report Says," *Miami Herald,* April 13, 2016, http://www.miamiherald.com/news/health-care /article71640637.html.

71 **In a *New York Times* article from 2015:** Richard Schiffman, "Wary of Mainstream Medicine, Immigrants Seek Remedies from Home," *The New York Times,* November 13, 2015, https://www.nytimes.com/2015/11/15 /nyregion/wary-of-mainstream-medicine-immigrants-seek-remedies -from-home.html.

72 **It is difficult to know how many botanicas:** Anahí Viladrich, "Botánicas in America's Backyard: Uncovering the World of Latino Healers' Herb-healing Practices in New York City," *Human Organization* 65, no. 4 (Winter 2006): 407–19 (p. 409).

75 **I am generally unfriendly toward institutionalized:** Mambo Chita Tann, *Haitian Vodou: An Introduction to Haiti's Indigenous Spiritual Tradition* (Woodbury, Minn.: Llewellyn Publications, 2012); Alfred Métraux, *Voodoo in Haiti* (Pickle Partners Publishing, 2016), .

76 **During my first visit to Miami:** Lizette Alvarez, "58,000 Haitians in U.S. May Lose Post-Earthquake Protections," *The New York Times,* May 20,

2017, https://www.nytimes.com/2017/05/20/us/haitians-us-earthquake
-immigration-protections.html.

76 **The wait period before TPS:** Martin Vassolo, "Scared to Death: Miami
Haitians Fear Family Separations if Protected Status Expires," *Miami Herald*, July 24, 2018.

79 **"some very fine people on both sides":** Rosie Gray, "Trump Defends
White-Nationalist Protesters: 'Some Very Fine People on Both Sides,'"
The Atlantic, August 15, 2017, https://www.theatlantic.com/politics/archive
/2017/08/trump-defends-white-nationalist-protesters-some-very-fine
-people-on-both-sides/537012/.

82 **They have been marching for forty years:** Uki Goñi, "40 Years Later,
the Mothers of Argentina's 'Disappeared' Refuse to Be Silent," *The Guardian*, April 28, 2017, https://www.theguardian.com/world/2017/apr/28
/mothers-plaza-de-mayo-argentina-anniversary.

85 **This sounds to me like a notario:** Rick Bowmer, "Legal Experts Warn
Immigrant Families: Beware of 'Notario' Scams," NBC News, November
30, 2014, https://www.nbcnews.com/news/latino/legal-experts-warn
-immigrant-families-beware-notario-scams-n256671.

87 **Vodou spirits are said to protect and nurture queer people:** Beenish
Ahmed, "Queer Haitians Find a Refuge in Vodou," *The Advocate*, October 31,
2016, https://www.advocate.com/current-issue/2016/10/31/why-queer
-haitians-are-turning-vodou.

94 **In 1995, Bill Clinton introduced a revision:** Richard Steven Conley,
"Cuba," in *Historical Dictionary of the Clinton Era* (Plymouth, UK: Scarecrow Press, 2012), p. 55.

94 **If they were detained in the crossing:** Julia Preston, "Tension Simmers
as Cubans Breeze Across U.S. Border," *The New York Times*, February 12,
2016, https://www.nytimes.com/2016/02/13/us/as-cubans-and-central
-americans-enter-us-the-welcomes-vary.html.

94 **Barack Obama ended the policy:** Alan Gomez, "Obama Ends 'Wet Foot,
Dry Foot' Policy for Cubans," *USA Today*, January 12, 2017, https://www
.usatoday.com/story/news/world/2017/01/12/obama-ends-wet-foot-dry
-foot-policy-cubans/96505172/.

CHAPTER 4: Flint

99 **I first visited Flint in 2017:** Associated Press, "Another Official Facing
Manslaughter Charge in Flint Water," WTOP.com, October 9, 2017,
https://wtop.com/business-finance/2017/10/another-official-to-face
-manslaughter-charge-in-flint-water/.

99 **Throughout the 1990s, General Motors:** Keith Bradsher, "G.M. to Close
Car Factory, Delivering Big Blow to Flint," *The New York Times*, November 22, 1997, https://www.nytimes.com/1997/11/22/business/gm-to
-close-car-factory-delivering-big-blow-to-flint.html; Peter Bourque, "Re-

membering When GM Employed Half of Flint, Michigan," *Arizona Daily Star*, August 2, 2009, https://tucson.com/lifestyles/remembering-when -gm-employed-half-of-flint-michigan/article_e4176079–2b6b-591e -bd13–3ca041c9dcf2.html.

99 **By 2014, half of the population had left:** Anna Clark, "Flint Prepares to Be Left Behind Once More," *The New Republic*, March 3, 2016, https:// newrepublic.com/article/131015/flint-prepares-left-behind.

99 **Fewer than one hundred thousand people:** United States Census Bureau, "Flint City, Michigan, V2017," https://www.census.gov/quickfacts /fact/table/flintcitymichigan/PST045217.

100 **In 2016, 45 percent of Flint:** Dominic Adams, "Here's How Flint Went from Boom Town to Nation's Highest Poverty Rate," *MLive*, September 21, 2017, updated January 19, 2019, https://www.mlive.com/news/flint /index.ssf/2017/09/heres_how_flint_went_from_boom.html.

100 **One out of nine houses in Flint is vacant:** Anna Clark, "Flint, Michigan Has an Ambitious New Plan to Fight Blight," *Next City*, March 16, 2015, https://nextcity.org/daily/entry/flint-michigan-blight-plan-cost-metrics.

100 **When President Obama declared a state of emergency:** Tony Dukoupil, "National Guard Deployed in Flint Water Crisis," MSNBC, January 13, 2016, updated January 27, 2016, http://www.msnbc.com/msnbc/national -guard-deployed-flint-water-crisis.

100 **They had seen reports of the poisoned water:** Erica Hellerstein, "The Forgotten Victims of the Flint Water Crisis," *Think Progress*, January 28, 2016, https://thinkprogress.org/the-forgotten-victims-of-the-flint-water -crisis-c57395f2983e/.

105 **Research has found that exposure to lead:** "Lead Poisoning Effects," Mt. Washington Pediatric Hospital, http://www.mwph.org/programs/lead -treatment/effects.

106 **"So lukewarm and cold-water showers":** United States Environmental Protection Agency, "Basic Information About Lead in Drinking Water," EPA.gov, accessed August 2, 2018, https://www.epa.gov/ground-water -and-drinking-water/basic-information-about-lead-drinking-water.

112 **I come back to Flint almost a year later:** Jacey Fortin, "Michigan Will No Longer Provide Free Bottled Water to Flint," *The New York Times*, April 8, 2018, https://www.nytimes.com/2018/04/08/us/flint-water -bottles.html.

112 **even though they've replaced only sixty-two hundred pipes:** Adrienne Mahsa Varkiani, "Michigan Won't Give Flint Free Bottled Water, Even Though Lead Pipes Are Still in Use," *Think Progress*, April 8, 2018, https:// thinkprogress.org/michigan-wont-give-flint-free-bottled-water-d959e 535b79b/.

118 **shoot and shoot and shoot shoot and shoot:** Michael Cooper, "Officers in Bronx Fire 41 Shots, and an Unarmed Man Is Killed," *The New York*

Times, February 5, 1999, https://www.nytimes.com/1999/02/05/nyregion /officers-in-bronx-fire-41-shots-and-an-unarmed-man-is-killed.html.

CHAPTER 5: Cleveland

123 **A Vietnam War vet threw a tantrum:** Daniel L. Young, "We Were Never Welcomed Home in Willard," *Norwalk Reflector,* March 22, 2017, http:// www.norwalkreflector.com/Letter-to-the-Editor/2017/03/22/Forum -Young.

124 **At a city meeting dedicated to planning the party:** Miriam Jordan, "One Ohio Town's Immigration Clash, Down in the Actual Muck," *The New York Times,* June 18, 2017, https://www.nytimes.com/2017/06/18 /us/willard-ohio-migrant-workers.html.

124 **The city has a population of approximately:** United States Census Bureau, "Quick Facts: Willard city, Ohio, V2017," https://www.census.gov /quickfacts/fact/table/willardcityohio/PST045217.

131 **One study found that family income:** Migration Policy Institute, "Deportation of a Parent Can Have Significant and Long-Lasting Harmful Effects on Child Well-Being, as a Pair of Reports from MPI and the Urban Institute Detail," Migration Policy Institute, September 21, 2015, https:// www.migrationpolicy.org/news/deportation-parent-can-have-significant -and-long-lasting-harmful-effects-child-well-being-pair.

131 **Another study found that American-citizen children:** Lisseth Rojas-Flores, Mari L. Clements, Josephine Hwang Koo, and Judy London, "Trauma and Psychological Distress in Latino Citizen Children Following Parental Detention and Deportation," *Psychological Trauma: Theory, Research, Practice, and Policy* 9, no. 3 (May 2017): 352–61.

132 **There are no clowns in fields:** Nina Shapiro, "A Washington County That Went for Trump Is Shaken as Immigrant Neighbors Start Disappearing," *The Seattle Times,* November 9, 2017, updated November 15, 2017, https:// www.seattletimes.com/seattle-news/northwest/fear-regrets-as-pacific -county-residents-go-missing-amid-immigration-crackdown-police-chief -neighbors-kind-of-in-shock-after-immigration-arrests-in-pacific-county -immigration-crack/.

136 **They're wearing ankle monitors given to them:** Colleen Long, Frank Bajak, and Will Weissert, "ICE Issuing More Immigrant Ankle Monitors. But Do They Work?" Associated Press, August 25, 2018, https://www .apnews.com/dfcdc6302e154753a526c04706df45d6.

137 **There was an ancient Greek belief:** Benjamin Woodring, "Liberty to Misread: Sanctuary and Possibility in *The Comedy of Errors,*" *Yale Journal of Law and the Humanities* 28, no. 2 (2016).

138 **A few months later, Carter:** Bill Keller, "Kevin Carter, a Pulitzer Winner for Sudan Photo, Is Dead at 33," *The New York Times,* July 29, 1994.

142 **In 1996, the IRS even made a special provision:** https://www.american immigrationcouncil.org/research/facts-about-individual-tax-identification -number-itin.

CHAPTER 6: New Haven

154 **Even though half of undocumented people:** Alexia Fernández Campbell, "Trump Says Undocumented Immigrants Are an Economic Burden. They Pay Billions in Taxes," *Vox*, updated October 25, 2018, https://www .vox.com/2018/4/13/17229018/undocumented-immigrants-pay-taxes.

154 **According to the Migration Policy Institute:** Migration Policy Institute, "Profile of the Unauthorized Population: United States," https://www .migrationpolicy.orgzdata/unauthorized-immigrant-population/state/US.

160 **he found his subjects suffered:** Karla Cornejo Villavicencio, "The Psychic Toll of Trump's DACA Decision," *The New York Times*, September 8, 2017, https://www.nytimes.com/2017/09/08/opinion/sunday/mental-health -daca.html.

160 **people forming human chains to block ICE officers:** Elisha Fieldstadt, "ICE Came for Their Neighbor, so These Tennesseans Formed a Human Chain to Protect Him," NBC News, July 23, 2019, https://www.nbcnews .com/news/us-news/ice-tries-detain-man-tennessee-home-neighbors -form-human-chain-n1032791?fbclid=IwAR3PPeOXZY6fZ1QqQI1Ylnk 4uXDGsLQWECR9vKIw7MVaqRa0QQNooWX0788.

168 **This all changed recently, when reports:** Viviana Andazola Marquez, "I Accidentally Turned My Dad In to Immigration Services," *The New York Times*, October 24, 2017, https://www.nytimes.com/2017/10/24 /opinion/ice-detained-father-yale.html; Noah Lanard, "Married Immigrants Seeking Green Cards Are Now Targets for Deportation," *Mother Jones*, April 20, 2018, https://www.motherjones.com/politics/2018/04/married -immigrants-seeking-green-cards-are-now-targets-for-deportation/.

KARLA CORNEJO VILLAVICENCIO has written about immigration, music, beauty, and mental illness for *The New York Times*, *The Atlantic*, *The New Republic*, *Glamour*, *Elle*, *Vogue*, *n+1*, and *The New Inquiry*, among others. She is a doctoral candidate at Yale and lives in New Haven with her partner and dog.